BY SUSAN SONTAG

FICTION

The Benefactor • *Death Kit* • *I, etcetera*
The Way We Live Now • *The Volcano Lover* • *In America*

ESSAYS

Against Interpretation • *Styles of Radical Will*
On Photography • *Illness As Metaphor* • *Under the Sign of Saturn*
AIDS and Its Metaphors • *Where the Stress Falls*
Regarding the Pain of Others

FILM SCRIPTS

Duet for Cannibals • *Brother Carl*

PLAY

Alice in Bed

A Susan Sontag Reader

At the Same Time

Susan Sontag

·

At the Same Time

ESSAYS AND SPEECHES

·

Edited by Paolo Dilonardo and Anne Jump

Foreword by David Rieff

Farrar Straus Giroux   New York

Farrar, Straus and Giroux
19 Union Square West, New York 10003

Copyright © 2007 by The Estate of Susan Sontag
Preface and compilation copyright © 2007 by
Paolo Dilonardo and Anne Jump
Foreword copyright © 2007 by David Rieff
All rights reserved
Distributed in Canada by Douglas & McIntyre Ltd.
Printed in the United States of America
First edition, 2007

Library of Congress Cataloging-in-Publication Data
Sontag, Susan, 1933–2004.
At the same time : essays and speeches / Susan Sontag ; edited by Paolo
Dilonardo and Anne Jump ; with a foreword by David Rieff.—1st ed.
    p.   cm.
ISBN-13: 978-0-374-10072-8 (hardcover : alk. paper)
ISBN-10: 0-374-10072-1 (harcover : alk. paper)
I. Dilonardo, Paolo.   II. Jump, Anne.   III. Title.

PS3569.O6547A93 2007
814'.54—dc22

                                                    2006031179

Designed by Dorothy Schmiderer Baker

www.fsgbooks.com

1   3   5   7   9   10   8   6   4   2

Contents

Contents

•

•

Preface

What follows on these pages is a work that Susan Sontag was actively outlining and planning in the last years of her life. Among other projects—including a third, more autobiographical book on illness, a novel set in Japan, and a collection of stories—she intended to publish a new collection of essays, "my last one," as she used to say, before returning to fiction.

Sontag had prepared various drafts of a table of contents, arranging the pieces she had written since the publication of *Where the Stress Falls* and leaving space for a few essays that she had plans to write, notably one on aphoristic thinking, a subject she had been interested in for some time, as future publications of her notebooks will show. Aside from those unwritten essays, however, this volume is as close as possible to the book she meant to publish.

While we cannot know what on these pages she would have rewritten (and she would have found much to revise, undoubtedly), we have prepared these essays in precisely the manner in which we so often worked with Susan Sontag. Throughout this book, we have endeavored to restore the original version of those pieces where the published version was cut or edited at the time of first publication. We have followed the order outlined in her notes for this collection, and we have incorporated her successive corrections to the essays and the edits she made in approved foreign editions.

.

Opening with a piece on beauty in which Sontag argues for the inextricability of ethic and aesthetic values, the first section forms the part of this book that she referred to as "Forwarding" in one draft of her table of contents and is comprised of the essays she wrote as introductions to works of literature in translation. The introductions were all published prior to the books they accompanied and were therefore edited repeatedly by Sontag, with the exception of the essay on Halldór Laxness, which she was revising as late as December 2004. Read together, these portraits and appreciations of admired writers have much in common: the celebration of Russian literature and its themes, from Tsvetayeva and Pasternak to Dostoyevsky and Leonid Tsypkin's "extraordinary mental tour of Russian reality"; the solitary nature of fiction-writing, from Tsypkin's writing "for the drawer" to Anna Banti's amorous dance with her character; the "journey of the soul" shared by the correspondents in 1926 and revealed in the works of Tsypkin, Banti, Serge, and Laxness; and, above all, the ongoing and self-revealing meditation on the art of storytelling, on the "truth of fiction," on "how to narrate and to what end," and on a particular subgenre of the novel, "a retelling of the life of a real person of accomplishment from another era."

.

The first three pieces of the second section are political pieces on the aftermath of September 11th and on the "war on terrorism." The first, written just days after the attacks, was published in a slightly different version by *The New Yorker*; the version that appears here is the original, and it is the text that was published in translation in many foreign countries. The second, a companion to and a reflection on the first, appears here for the first time in English. The third piece returns to these same questions one year after the attacks. This is the first time all three essays have appeared together in print.

The second half of this section is comprised of two pieces on photography, a coda, in a way, to *Regarding the Pain of Others*—the first, a short collection of musings on the subject, and the second, a searing analysis of the Abu Ghraib scandal, the response of the Bush administration, and the shift in American culture toward what Sontag termed an "increasing acceptance of brutality."

The last years of Sontag's life were ones of ongoing political engagement, as these pieces of journalism show. This was something she wrestled with, but as much as she wanted to find time to work on her book projects, and fiction in particular, world events prompted her to respond, to take action and urge others to do the same. She participated because she couldn't *not* participate.

.

In those same years, Sontag's literary work and political activism brought her increasing international recognition. She was awarded a number of prizes, including the Jerusalem Prize, the Friedenspreis, the Prince of Asturias Award, and the Los Angeles Public Library Literary Award, and was asked to deliver lectures at commencement exercises, universities, and book fairs around the world. The third section is a collection of some of the speeches Sontag gave at these events. In these speeches, her public voice, while expanding on the main literary and political themes of the first and second sections of this book, reflects on its role as such and enters in a compelling dialogue with the voice of the writer, championing the task and enterprise of literature (and translation), and revealing glimpses of the life of a militant reader and a passionate member of the republic of letters.

•

Susan Sontag did not have a working title for the collection she was preparing. We have chosen *At the Same Time*, the title of the last speech she gave, as a tribute to the polyphonic quality of this book, to the inseparability in her work of literature and politics, aesthetics and ethics, inner and outer life.

—*Paolo Dilonardo and Anne Jump*

Foreword

In thinking of my mother now, more than a year after her death, I often find myself dwelling on that startling phrase in Auden's great memorial poem for Yeats—words that both sum up what small immortality artistic accomplishment sometimes can confer and are, simultaneously, such an extraordinary euphemism for extinction. Once dead, Yeats, Auden writes, "became his admirers."

Loved ones, admirers, detractors, works, work: beyond soon-to-be-distorted or at least edited memories, beyond the possessions soon to be dispersed or distributed, beyond libraries, archives, voice recordings, videotape, and photographs—that is surely the most that can ever remain of a life, no matter how well and kindly lived, no matter how accomplished.

I have known many writers who assuaged themselves about mortality, to the extent they could, with at least the fantasy that their work would outlive them and also the lives of those of their loved ones who would keep faith with memory for whatever time remained to *them*. My mother was one such writer, working with one eye imaginatively cocked toward posterity. I should add that, given her unalloyed fear of extinction—in no part of her, even in the last agonized days of her ending, was there the slightest ambivalence, the slightest acceptance—the thought was not just scant consolation, it was no consolation. She did not want to leave. I do not pretend to know much about what she felt as she lay dying, three months in two successive beds in two successive hospital rooms, as her body became almost one huge sore, but this at least I can assert confidently.

What else can I say? Personally, a lot, of course, but I do not propose to do so. So in this writing, let me be one of those admirers and not a son, and introduce this last collection of her essays that she herself largely selected and shaped in her lifetime. Had she gained even some small, life-extending remission from her blood cancer, I am sure she would have added to this book, amended the essays (there was never a book she published where she did not do this), and doubtless made cuts as well. Fiercely proud of her work, she was also a stern critic of it. But these changes were for her to make, certainly not for me in the role of admirer. There will be other works by Susan Sontag published in the next few years—diaries, letters, uncollected essays—and these will be shaped by my hand and by the hands of some others. But not here, not now. This time, this last time, it is possible for me to know and thus fully honor her intentions.

Even in doing so, though, I am all too aware that the fact that this is her last book gives it a specific gravity it would not have had otherwise. Inescapably, it will be read as a summing-up, as her final words. That she did not mean these to be her final words, that, before her illness stripped her of her identity as a writer (as it did, horribly, well before she died), she was full of plans for other writings, above all for stories and a new novel, will do little to alter this impression. And not wrongly; the themes of the essays and speeches in this book do, I think, fairly represent many, though not by any means all, of the questions—political, literary, intellectual, and moral—that my mother cared most about.

She was interested in everything. Indeed, if I had only one word with which to evoke her, it would be *avidity*. She wanted to experience everything, taste everything, go everywhere, do everything. Even travel, she once wrote, she conceived of as accumulation. And her apartment, which was a kind of reification of the contents of her head, was filled almost to bursting with an amazingly disparate collection of objects, prints, photographs, and, of course, books, endless books. If anything, the gamut of her interests was what was hard (for me at least) to fathom, impossible to keep up with. In her story "Project for a Trip to China," she wrote:

> Three things I've been promising myself for twenty years that I would do before I die:
> —climb the Matterhorn
> —learn to play the harpsichord
> —study Chinese

In another story, "Debriefing," she wrote: "We know more than we can use. Look at all this stuff I've got in my head: rockets and Venetian churches, David Bowie and Diderot, nuoc mam and Big Macs, sunglasses and orgasms."

And then she added, "And we don't know nearly enough." I think that, for her, the joy of living and the joy of knowing really were one and the same. In my admirer guise, this is what I take from so much of her work, including this book.

I used to tease my mother by saying to her that though she had largely kept her own biography out of her work, her essays of appreciation—on Roland Barthes, on Walter Benjamin, on Elias Canetti, to name three of the best of them—were more self-revealing than she perhaps imagined. At the very least, they were idealizations. At the time, she laughed, lightly assenting. But I was never sure whether she agreed or not, nor am I now. I was taken back to such conversations when, in the essay "An Argument About Beauty," included in this volume, I came upon the sentence that reads: "Beauty is part of the history of idealizing, which is itself part of the history of consolation."

Did she write in order to console herself? I believe so, though this is more intuition than grounded judgment. Beauty, I know, was a consolation for her, whether she found it on the walls of museums to which she was such an ardent and inveterate visitor, in the temples of Japan that she so adored, in serious music, which was the virtually nonstop accompaniment to her evenings at home while working, and in the eighteenth-century prints on the walls of her apartment. "The capacity to be overwhelmed by the beautiful," she writes in the same essay, "is astonishingly sturdy and survives amidst the harshest distractions." I would speculate that here she is thinking of that harshest of all the distractions that claimed her in life, her illnesses, the two bouts of cancer that wracked her but that she survived (obviously, this essay was written before she developed cancer for the third and last time).

Foreword

It is sometimes said of my mother's work that she was torn between aestheticism and moralism, beauty and ethics. Any intelligent reader of hers will see the force of this, but I think a shrewder account would emphasize their inseparability in her work. "The wisdom that becomes available over a profound, lifelong engagement with the aesthetic," she wrote, "cannot, I venture to say, be duplicated by any other kind of seriousness." I do not know if this is true. I do know that she believed this with every fiber of herself, and that her almost devotional insistence on never missing a concert, an exhibition, an opera, or a ballet was for her an act of loyalty to seriousness, not an indulgence, and a part of her project as a writer, not a taste, let alone an addiction.

Where it led her was to a kind of "devotee-ship." She excelled in admiration. In another essay in this volume, "1926 . . . ,"a meditation on Pasternak, Tsvetayeva, and Rilke, she describes the three poets as participants in the sacred delirium of art, of a god (Rilke), and of his two Russian worshippers whom, she writes, "we, the readers of their letters, know to be future gods." The appropriateness of such worship was, for my mother, self-evident, and she practiced it until she could no longer practice anything at all, so much was it second nature to her. This is what her essays of admiration are all about. It is also why, though she valued her work as a fiction writer far more than anything else she did, she could not stop writing them—as this book shows one last time.

In the run-up to the stem cell transplant that was her last, thin chance for survival, she would speak of her failure to write the novels and stories she had wanted to do, some of which are mapped out in her diaries and workbooks. And yet when I asked her once why she had devoted so much time to making essayistic cases for writers ranging from Nathalie Sarraute at the beginning of her career to Leonid Tsypkin, Halldór Laxness, and Anna Banti in the year she got ill (these pieces are collected in this volume), what she once called "the evangelical incentive" she spoke of as a duty, whereas fiction writing alone had brought her pleasure as a writer. But she was never able to think of herself as a writer alone, and in the essay on Banti she speaks of "militant reading." It was that militant reader, or, as she put it elsewhere, the would-be "world-improver," I believe, who wrote most of the essays, while the fiction languished. She knew it, of course. On her seventieth birthday, she told me that what she most yearned for was time, time to do the work that essay writing had distracted her from so often and so lengthily. And as she grew sicker, she spoke with leaden sadness of time wasted. To the end, writing of Victor Serge (that piece, too, is collected here), she identified herself with what she thought of as a previous era defined by "its introspective energies and passionate intellectual quests and code of self-sacrifice and immense hope." That irony-less commitment always made my mother's detractors rail at her. But irony or world-weariness would never have gotten a bookish, asthmatic girl from a family in which learning was not greatly prized through a girlhood in southern Arizona and suburban Los Angeles. "What saved me as a schoolchild in Arizona," she wrote, "waiting to grow up, waiting to escape into a larger reality, was reading books . . . To have access to literature, world literature, was to escape the prison of national vanity, of philistinism, of compulsory provincialism, of inane schooling, of imperfect destinies and bad luck."

I think she survived by taking herself with the fierce seriousness that so put her detractors off. Certainly, she felt from start to finish that to let up, to relax, would mean to falter. In her essay on Canetti, she quotes approvingly his remark, "I try to imagine someone telling Shakespeare to relax." My mother knew how to play for keeps.

What she did not know how to do was to wall herself off from her own extraliterary commitments, above all her political involvements from Vietnam to Iraq. Much as I admire her piece on the torture photographs from Abu Ghraib (also included here along with some speeches and an interview on the so-called war on terrorism, Israel-Palestine, and Iraq), I wish it had not been the last major piece of work she undertook. I wish . . . Well, I wish she had written a short story. She herself was the first to insist that she did not hold her political opinions "as a writer," adding that "the influence a writer can exert is purely adventitious," that it was now "an aspect of the culture of celebrity."

But it was not only the activist in herself that my mother viewed with misgiving. In this volume, as she did so often in her work, she returned again and again not to her life as a writer but to her life as a reader. In her essay on translation, "The World as India," she notes, "A writer is first of all a reader. It is from reading that I derive the standards by which I measure my own work and according to which I fall lamentably short. It is from reading, even before writing, that I became part of a community—the community of literature—which includes more dead than living writers." Now she has joined them. Now she has become her admirers. Much as I wish, wish beyond cogent expression, that it were otherwise. Reader, over to you.

—*David Rieff*

An Argument About Beauty

Responding at last, in April 2002, to the scandal created by the revelation of innumerable cover-ups of sexually predatory priests, Pope John Paul II told the American cardinals summoned to the Vatican, "A great work of art may be blemished, but its beauty remains; and this is a truth which any intellectually honest critic will recognize."

Is it too odd that the pope likens the Catholic Church to a great—that is, beautiful—work of art? Perhaps not, since the inane comparison allows him to turn abhorrent misdeeds into something like the scratches in the print of a silent film or craquelure covering the surface of an Old Master painting, blemishes that we reflexively screen out or see past. The pope likes venerable ideas. And beauty, as a term signifying (like health) an indisputable excellence, has been a perennial resource in the issuing of peremptory evaluations.

Permanence, however, is not one of beauty's more obvious attributes; and the contemplation of beauty, when it is expert, may be wreathed in pathos, the drama on which Shakespeare elaborates in many of the sonnets. Traditional celebrations of beauty in Japan, like the annual rite of cherry-blossom viewing, are keenly elegiac; the most stirring beauty is the most evanescent. To make beauty in some sense imperishable required a lot of conceptual tinkering and transposing, but the idea was simply too alluring, too potent, to be squandered on the praise of superior embodiments. The aim was to multiply the notion, to allow for kinds of beauty, beauty with adjectives, arranged on a scale of ascending value and incorruptibility, with the metaphorized uses ("intellectual beauty," "spiritual beauty") taking precedence over what ordinary language extols as beautiful—a gladness to the senses.

The less "uplifting" beauty of face and body remains the most commonly visited site of the beautiful. But one would hardly expect the pope to invoke *that* sense of beauty while constructing an exculpatory account of several generations' worth of the clergy's sexual molestation of children and protection of the molesters. More to the point—his point—is the "higher" beauty of art. However much art may seem to be a matter of surface and reception by the senses, it has generally been accorded an honorary citizenship in the domain of "inner" (as opposed to "outer") beauty. Beauty, it seems, is immutable, at least when incarnated—fixed—in the form of art, because it is in art that beauty as an idea, an eternal idea, is best embodied. Beauty (should you choose to use the word that way) is deep, not superficial; hidden, sometimes, rather than obvious; consoling, not troubling; indestructible, as in art, rather than ephemeral, as in nature. Beauty, the stipulatively uplifting kind, perdures.

.

The best theory of beauty is its history. Thinking about the history of beauty means focusing on its deployment in the hands of specific communities.

Communities dedicated by their leaders to stemming what is perceived as a noxious tide of innovative views have no interest in modifying the bulwark provided by the use of beauty as unexceptionable commendation and consolation. It is not surprising that John Paul II—and the preserve-and-conserve institution for which he speaks—feels as comfortable with beauty as with the idea of the good.

It also seems inevitable that when, almost a century ago, the most prestigious communities concerned with the fine arts dedicated themselves to drastic projects of innovation, beauty would turn up on the front line of notions to be discredited. Beauty could not but appear a conservative standard to the makers and proclaimers of the new; Gertrude Stein said that to call a work of art beautiful means that it is dead. Beautiful has come to mean "merely" beautiful: there is no more vapid or philistine compliment.

Elsewhere, beauty still reigns, irrepressible. (How could it not?) When that notorious beauty-lover Oscar Wilde announced in *The Decay of Lying*, "Nobody of any real culture . . . ever talks nowadays about the beauty of a sunset. Sunsets are quite old fashioned," sunsets reeled under the blow, then recovered. *Les beaux arts*, when summoned to a similar call to be up to date, did not. The subtraction of beauty as a standard for art hardly signals a decline of the authority of beauty. Rather, it testifies to a decline in the belief that there is something called art.

·

Even when beauty was an unquestioned criterion of value in the arts, it was defined laterally, by evoking some other quality that was supposed to be the essence or sine qua non of something that was beautiful. A definition of the beautiful was no more (or less) than a commendation of the beautiful. When, for example, Lessing equated beauty with harmony, he was offering another general idea of what is excellent or desirable.

In the absence of a definition in the strict sense, there was supposed to be an organ or capacity for registering beauty (that is, value) in the arts, called "taste," and a canon of works discerned by people of taste, seekers after more rarefied gratifications, adepts of connoisseurship. For in the arts—unlike life—beauty was not assumed to be necessarily apparent, evident, obvious.

The problem with taste was that, however much it resulted in periods of large agreement within communities of art lovers, it issued from private, immediate, and revocable responses to art. And the consensus, however firm, was never more than local. To address this defect, Kant—a dedicated universalizer—proposed a distinctive faculty of "judgment" with discernible principles of a general and abiding kind; the tastes legislated by this faculty of judgment, if properly reflected upon, should be the possession of all. But "judgment" did not have its intended effect of shoring up "taste" or making it, in a certain sense, more democratic. For one thing, taste-as-principled-judgment was hard to apply, since it had the most tenuous connection with the actual works of art deemed incontestably great or beautiful, unlike the pliable, empirical criterion of taste. And taste is now a far weaker, more assailable notion than it was in the late eighteenth century. *Whose* taste? Or, more insolently, *who* sez?

As the relativistic stance in cultural matters pressed harder on the old assessments, definitions of beauty—descriptions of its essence—became emptier. Beauty could no longer be something as positive as harmony. For Valéry, the nature of beauty is that it cannot be defined; beauty is precisely "the ineffable."

The failure of the notion of beauty reflects the discrediting of the prestige of judgment itself, as something that could conceivably be impartial or objective, not always self-serving or self-referring. It also reflects the discrediting of binary discourses in the arts. Beauty defines itself as the antithesis of the ugly. Obviously, you can't say something is beautiful if you're not willing to say something is ugly. But there are more and more taboos about calling something, anything, ugly. (For an explanation, look first not at the rise of so-called "political correctness," but at the evolving ideology of consumerism, then at the complicity between these two.) The point is to find what is beautiful in what has not hitherto been regarded as beautiful (or: the beautiful in the ugly).

Similarly, there is more and more resistance to the idea of "good taste," that is, to the dichotomy good taste/bad taste, except for occasions that allow one to celebrate the defeat of snobbery and the triumph of what was once condescended to as bad taste. Today, good taste seems even more retrograde an idea than beauty. Austere, difficult "modernist" art and literature have come to seem old-fashioned, a conspiracy of snobs. Innovation is relaxation now; today's E-Z Art gives the green light to all. In the cultural climate favoring the more user-friendly art of recent years, the beautiful seems, if not obvious, then pretentious. Beauty continues to take a battering in what are called, absurdly, our culture wars.

.

That beauty applied to some things and not to others, that it was a principle of *discrimination*, was once its strength and its appeal. Beauty belonged to the family of notions that establish rank, and accorded well with a social order unapologetic about station, class, hierarchy, and the right to exclude.

What had been a virtue of the concept became its liability. Beauty, which once seemed vulnerable because it was too general, loose, porous, was revealed as—on the contrary— excluding too much. Discrimination, once a positive faculty (meaning refined judgment, high standards, fastidiousness), turned negative: it meant prejudice, bigotry, blindness to the virtues of what was not identical with oneself.

The strongest, most successful move against beauty was in the arts: beauty—and the caring about beauty—was restrictive; as the current idiom has it, elitist. Our appreciations, it was felt, could be so much more inclusive if we said that something, instead of being beautiful, was "interesting."

Of course, when people said a work of art was interesting, this did not mean that they necessarily liked it—much less that they thought it beautiful. It usually meant no more than they thought they ought to like it. Or that they liked it, sort of, even though it wasn't beautiful.

Or they might describe something as interesting to avoid the banality of calling it beautiful. Photography was the art where "the interesting" first triumphed, and early on: the new, photographic way of seeing proposed everything as a potential subject for the camera. The beautiful could not have yielded such a range of subjects; and it soon came to seem uncool to boot as a judgment. Of a photograph of a sunset, a beautiful sunset, anyone with minimal standards of verbal sophistication might well prefer to say, "Yes, the photograph is interesting."

.

What is interesting? Mostly, what has not previously been thought beautiful (or good). The sick are interesting, as Nietzsche points out. The wicked, too. To name something as interesting implies challenging old orders of praise; such judgments aspire to be found insolent or at least ingenious. Connoisseurs of "the interesting"—whose antonym is "the boring"—appreciate clash, not harmony. Liberalism is boring, declares Carl Schmitt in *The Concept of the Political*, written in 1932. (The following year he joined the Nazi Party.) A politics conducted according to liberal principles lacks drama, flavor, conflict, while strong autocratic politics— and war—are interesting.

Long use of "the interesting" as a criterion of value has, inevitably, weakened its transgressive bite. What is left of the old insolence lies mainly in its disdain for the consequences of actions and of judgments. As for the truthfulness of the ascription—that does not even enter the story. One calls something interesting precisely so as not to have to commit to a judgment of beauty (or of goodness). The interesting is now mainly a consumerist concept, bent on enlarging its domain: the more things become interesting, the more the marketplace grows. The boring—understood as an absence, an emptiness—implies its antidote: the promiscuous, empty affirmations of the interesting. It is a peculiarly inconclusive way of experiencing reality.

In order to enrich this deprived take on our experiences, one would have to acknowledge a full notion of boredom: depression, rage (suppressed despair). Then one could work toward a full notion of the interesting. But that quality of experience—of feeling—one would probably no longer even *want* to call interesting.

•

Beauty can illustrate an ideal, a perfection. Or, because of its identification with women (more accurately, with Woman), it can trigger the usual ambivalence that stems from the age-old denigration of the feminine. Much of the discrediting of beauty needs to be understood as a result of the gender inflection. Misogyny, too, might underlie the urge to metaphorize beauty, thereby promoting it out of the realm of the "merely" feminine, the unserious, the specious. For if women are worshipped because they are beautiful, they are condescended to for their preoccupation with making or keeping themselves beautiful. Beauty is theatrical, it is for being looked at and admired; and the word is as likely to suggest the beauty industry (beauty magazines, beauty parlors, beauty products)—the theater of feminine frivolity—as the beauties of art and of nature. How else to explain the association of beauty—i.e., women—with mindlessness? To be concerned with one's own beauty is to risk the charge of narcissism and frivolity. Consider all the beauty synonyms, starting with the "lovely," the merely "pretty," which cry out for a virile transposition.

"Handsome is as handsome does." (But not: "Beautiful is as beautiful does.") Though it applies no less than does "beautiful" to appearance, "handsome"—free of associations with the feminine—seems a more sober, less gushing way of commending. Beauty is not ordinarily associated with gravitas. Thus one might prefer to call the vehicle for delivering searing images of war and atrocity a "handsome book," as I did in the preface to a compilation of photographs by Don McCullin, lest calling it a "beautiful book" (which it was) would seem an affront to its appalling subject.

·

It's usually assumed that beauty is, almost tautologically, an "aesthetic" category, which puts it, according to many, on a collision course with the ethical. But beauty, even beauty in the amoral mode, is never naked. And the ascription of beauty is never unmixed with moral values. Far from the aesthetic and the ethical being poles apart, as Kierkegaard and Tolstoy insisted, the aesthetic is itself a quasi-moral project. Arguments about beauty since Plato are stocked with questions about the proper relation to the beautiful (the irresistibly, enthrallingly beautiful), which is thought to flow from the nature of beauty itself.

The perennial tendency to make of beauty itself a binary concept, to split it up into "inner" and "outer," "higher" and "lower" beauty, is the usual way that judgments of the beautiful are colonized by moral judgments. From a Nietzschean (or

Wildean) point of view, this may be improper, but it seems to me unavoidable. And the wisdom that becomes available over a deep, lifelong engagement with the aesthetic cannot, I venture to say, be duplicated by any other kind of seriousness. Indeed, the various definitions of beauty come at least as close to a plausible characterization of virtue, and of a fuller humanity, as the attempts to define goodness as such.

•

Beauty is part of the history of idealizing, which is itself part of the history of consolation. But beauty may not always console. The beauty of face and figure torments, subjugates; that beauty is imperious. The beauty that is human, and the beauty that is made (art)—both raise the fantasy of possession. Our model of the disinterested comes from the beauty of nature—a nature that is distant, overarching, unpossessable.

From a letter written by a German soldier standing guard in the Russian winter in late December 1942:

> The most beautiful Christmas I had ever seen, made entirely of disinterested emotion and stripped of all tawdry trimmings. I was all alone beneath an enormous starred sky, and I can remember a tear running down my frozen cheek, a tear neither of pain nor of joy but of emotion created by intense experience.*

Unlike beauty, often fragile and impermanent, the capacity to be overwhelmed by the beautiful is astonishingly sturdy and

*Quoted in Stephen G. Fritz, *Frontsoldaten: The German Soldier in World War II* (Lexington: University Press of Kentucky, 1995), 130.

survives amidst the harshest distractions. Even war, even the prospect of certain death, cannot expunge it.

.

The beauty of art is better, "higher," according to Hegel, than the beauty of nature because it is made by human beings and is the work of the spirit. But the discerning of beauty in nature is also the result of traditions of consciousness, and of culture—in Hegel's language, of spirit.

The responses to beauty in art and to beauty in nature are interdependent. As Wilde pointed out, art does more than school us on how and what to appreciate in nature. (He was thinking of poetry and painting. Today the standards of beauty in nature are largely set by photography.) What is beautiful reminds us of nature as such—of what lies beyond the human and the made—and thereby stimulates and deepens our sense of the sheer spread and fullness of reality, inanimate as well as pulsing, that surrounds us all.

A happy by-product of this insight, if insight it is: beauty regains its solidity, its inevitability, as a judgment needed to make sense of a large portion of one's energies, affinities, and admirations; and the usurping notions appear ludicrous.

Imagine saying, "That sunset is interesting."

1926...

Pasternak, Tsvetayeva, Rilke

What is happening in 1926, when the three poets are writing to one another?

On May 12 Shostakovich's Symphony No. 1 in F Minor is heard for the first time, performed by the Leningrad Philharmonic; the composer is nineteen years old.

On June 10 the elderly Catalan architect Antonio Gaudí, on the walk he takes every day from the construction site of the Cathedral of the Sagrada Familia to a church in the same neighborhood in Barcelona for vespers, is hit by a trolley, lies unattended on the street (because, it's said, nobody recognizes him), and dies.

On August 6 Gertrude Ederle, nineteen years old, American, swims from Cap Gris-Nez, France, to Kingsdown, England, in fourteen hours and thirty-one minutes, becoming the first woman to swim the English Channel and the first woman competing in a major sport to best the male record-holder.

On August 23 the movie idol Rudolph Valentino dies of endocarditis and septicemia in a hospital in New York.

On September 3 a steel broadcasting tower (Funkturm), 138 meters high, with restaurant and panorama platform, is inaugurated in Berlin.

Some books: volume two of Hitler's *Mein Kampf*, Hart Crane's *White Buildings*, A. A. Milne's *Winnie-the-Pooh*, Viktor Shklovsky's *Third Factory*, Louis Aragon's *Le Paysan de Paris*, D. H. Lawrence's *The Plumed Serpent*, Hemingway's *The Sun Also Rises*, Agatha Christie's *The Murder of Roger Ackroyd*, T. E. Lawrence's *Seven Pillars of Wisdom*.

A few films: Fritz Lang's *Metropolis*,* Vsevolod Pudovkin's *Mother*, Jean Renoir's *Nana*, Herbert Brenon's *Beau Geste*.

Two plays: Bertolt Brecht's *Mann ist Mann* and Jean Cocteau's *Orphée*.

On December 6, Walter Benjamin arrives for a two-month stay in Moscow. He does not meet the thirty-six-year-old Boris Pasternak.

Pasternak has not seen Marina Tsvetayeva for four years. Since she left Russia in 1922, they have become each other's most cherished interlocutor, and Pasternak, tacitly acknowledging Tsvetayeva as the greater poet, has made her his first reader.

Tsvetayeva, who is thirty-four, is living in penury with her husband and two children in Paris.

Rilke, who is fifty-one, is dying of leukemia in a sanatorium in Switzerland.

---

*Metropolis was filmed in 1926, and it premiered in January 1927. (Editors' note.)

•

Letters: Summer 1926 is a portrait of the sacred delirium of art. There are three participants: a god and two worshippers, who are also worshippers of each other (and who we, the readers of their letters, know to be future gods).

A pair of young Russian poets, who have exchanged years of fervent letters about work and life, enter into correspondence with a great German poet who, for both, is poetry incarnate. These three-way love letters—and they are that— are an incomparable dramatization of ardor about poetry and about the life of the spirit.

They portray a domain of reckless feeling and purity of aspiration that it would be our loss to dismiss as "romantic."

The literatures written in German and in Russian have been particularly devoted to spiritual exaltation. Tsvetayeva and Pasternak know German, and Rilke has studied and attained a passable mastery of Russian—all three suffused by the dreams of literary divinity promulgated in these languages. The Russians, lovers of German poetry and music since childhood (the mothers of both were pianists), expect the greatest poet of the age to be someone writing in the language of Goethe and Hölderlin. And the German-language poet has had as a formative early love and mentor a writer, born in St. Petersburg, with whom he traveled twice to Russia, ever since which he has considered that country his true, spiritual homeland.

On the second of these trips, in 1900, Pasternak actually saw and probably was presented to the young Rilke.

Pasternak's father, the celebrated painter, was an esteemed acquaintance; Boris, the future poet, was ten years old. It is with the sacred memory of Rilke boarding a train with his lover Lou Andreas-Salomé—they remain, reverently, unnamed—that Pasternak begins *Safe Conduct* (1931), his supreme achievement in prose.

Tsvetayeva, of course, has never set eyes on Rilke.

All three poets are agitated by seemingly incompatible needs: for the most absolute solitude and for the most intense communion with another like-minded spirit. "My voice can ring out pure and clear only when absolutely solitary," Pasternak tells his father in a letter. Ardor inflected by intransigence drives all of Tsvetayeva's writings. In "Art in the Light of Conscience" (1932), she writes:

> The poet can have only one prayer: not to understand the unacceptable—let me not understand, so that I may not be seduced . . . let me not hear, so that I may not answer . . . The poet's only prayer is a prayer for deafness.

And the signature two-step of Rilke's life, as we know from his letters to a variety of correspondents, mostly women, is flight from intimacy and a bid for unconditional sympathy and understanding.

Although the younger poets announce themselves as acolytes, the letters quickly become an exchange of equals, a competition of affinities. To those familiar with the main branches of Rilke's grandiose, often stately correspondence, it may come as a surprise to find him responding in almost the same eager, jubilant tones as his two Russian admirers. But never has he had interlocutors of this caliber. The sovereign, didactic Rilke we know from the *Letters to a Young Poet*, written between 1903 and 1908, has disappeared. Here is only angelic conversation. Nothing to teach. Nothing to learn.

Opera is the only medium now in which it is still acceptable to rhapsodize. The duo that concludes Richard Strauss's *Ariadne auf Naxos*, whose libretto is by one of Rilke's contemporaries, Hugo von Hofmannsthal, offers a comparable effusiveness. We are surely more comfortable with the paean to love as rebirth and self-transformation sung by Ariadne and Bacchus than with the upsurges of amorous feeling declared by the three poets.

And these letters are not concluding duos. They are duos trying, and eventually failing, to be trios. What kind of possession of each other do the poets expect? How consuming and how exclusive is this kind of love?

The correspondence has begun, with Pasternak's father as the intermediary, between Rilke and Pasternak. Then Pasternak suggests to Rilke that he write to Tsvetayeva, and the situation becomes a correspondence *à trois*. Last to enter the lists, Tsvetayeva quickly becomes the igniting force, so powerful, so outrageous are her need, her boldness, her emotional nakedness. Tsvetayeva is the relentless one, outgalloping first Pasternak, then Rilke. Pasternak, who no longer knows what to demand of Rilke, retreats (and Tsvetayeva also calls a halt to *their* correspondence); Tsvetayeva can envisage an erotic, engulfing tie. Imploring Rilke to consent to a meeting, she succeeds only in driving him away. Rilke, in his turn, falls silent. (His last letter to her is on August 19.)

The flow of rhetoric reaches the precipice of the sublime and topples over into hysteria, anguish, dread.

But curiously, death seems quite unreal. How astonished

and shattered the Russians are when this "phenomenon of nature" (so they thought of Rilke) is in *some* sense no more. Silence should be full. Silence that now has the name of death seems too great a diminishment.

So the correspondence has to continue.

Tsvetayeva writes a letter to Rilke a few days after being told he has died at the end of December, and addresses a long prose ode to him ("Your Death") the following year. The manuscript of *Safe Conduct*, which Pasternak completes almost five years after Rilke's death, ends with a letter to Rilke. ("If you were alive, this is the letter I would send you today.") Leading the reader through a labyrinth of elliptical memoiristic prose to the core of the poet's inwardness, *Safe Conduct* is written under the sign of Rilke and, if only unconsciously, in competition with Rilke, being an attempt to match if not surpass *The Notebooks of Malte Laurids Brigge* (1910), Rilke's supreme achievement in prose.

Early in *Safe Conduct*, Pasternak speaks of living on and for those occasions when "a complete feeling burst into space with the whole extent of space before it." Never has a brief for the powers of lyric poetry been made so brilliantly, so rapturously, as in these letters. Poetry cannot be abandoned or renounced, once you are "the lyre's thrall," Tsvetayeva instructs Pasternak in a letter of July 1925. "With poetry, dear friend, as with love; no separation until it drops you."

Or until death intervenes. Tsvetayeva and Pasternak haven't suspected that Rilke was seriously ill. Learning that he has died, the two poets are incredulous: it seems, cosmically speaking, unjust. And fifteen years later Pasternak would be surprised and remorseful when he received the news of Tsvetayeva's suicide in August 1941. He hadn't, he admitted, grasped the inevitability of the doom that awaited her if she decided to return to the Soviet Union with her family, as she did in 1939.

Separation had made everything replete. What would Rilke and Tsvetayeva have said to each other had they actually met? We know what Pasternak *didn't* say to Tsvetayeva when they were briefly reunited after thirteen years, in June 1935, on the day he arrived in Paris in the nightmarish role of official Soviet delegate to the International Writers' Congress for the Defense of Culture: he didn't warn her not to come back, not to think of coming back, to Moscow.

Maybe the ecstasies channeled into this correspondence could only have been voiced in separateness, and in response to the ways in which they failed one another (as the greatest writers invariably demand too much of, and are failed by, readers). Nothing can dim the incandescence of those exchanges over a few months in 1926 when they were hurling themselves at one another, making their impossible, glorious demands. Today, when "all is drowning in Pharisaism"—the phrase is Pasternak's—their ardors and their tenacities feel like raft, beacon, beach.

Loving Dostoyevsky

The literature of the second half of the twentieth century is a much traversed field, and it seems unlikely that there are still masterpieces in major, intently patrolled languages waiting to be discovered. Yet some ten years ago, rifling through a bin of scruffy-looking used paperbacks outside a bookshop on London's Charing Cross Road, I came across just such a book, *Summer in Baden-Baden*, which I would include among the most beautiful, exalting, and original achievements of a century's worth of fiction and parafiction.

The reasons for the book's obscurity are not hard to fathom. To begin with, its author was not by profession a writer. Leonid Tsypkin was a doctor, a distinguished medical researcher, who published nearly a hundred papers in scientific journals in the Soviet Union and abroad. But—discard any comparison with Chekhov and Bulgakov—this Russian doctor-writer never saw a single page of his literary work published during his lifetime.

Censorship and its intimidations are only part of the story. Tsypkin's fiction was, to be sure, a poor candidate for official publication. But it did not circulate in samizdat either, for Tsypkin remained—out of pride, intractable gloom, unwillingness to risk being rejected by the unofficial literary establishment—wholly outside the independent or underground literary circles that flourished in Moscow in the 1960s and 1970s, the era when he was writing "for the drawer." For literature itself.

Actually, it is something of a miracle that *Summer in Baden-Baden* survived at all.

Leonid Tsypkin was born in 1926 in Minsk of Russian-Jewish parents, both physicians. The medical specialty of his mother, Vera Polyak, was pulmonary tuberculosis. His father, Boris Tsypkin, was an orthopedic surgeon, who was arrested at the start of the Great Terror, in 1934, on the usual fanciful charges and then released, through the intervention of an influential friend, after he tried to commit suicide by jumping down a prison stairwell. He returned home on a stretcher, with a broken back, but he did not become an invalid and went on with his surgical practice until his death (at sixty-four) in 1961. Two of Boris Tsypkin's sisters and a brother were also arrested during the Terror, and perished.

Minsk fell a week after the German invasion in 1941, and Boris Tsypkin's mother, another sister, and two little nephews were murdered in the ghetto. Boris Tsypkin, his wife, and fifteen-year-old Leonid owed their escape from the city to the chairman of a nearby collective farm, a grateful ex-patient, who ordered several barrels of pickles taken off a truck to accommodate the esteemed surgeon and his family.

A year later Leonid Tsypkin began his medical studies, and when the war was over, he returned with his parents to Minsk, where he graduated from medical school in 1947. In 1948 he married Natalya Michnikova, an economist. Mikhail, their only child, was born in 1950. By then Stalin's anti-Semitic campaign, launched the year before, was racking up victims, and Tsypkin hid out on the staff of a rural psychiatric hospital. In 1957 he was allowed to settle with his wife and son in Moscow, where he had been offered a post as a pathologist at the prestigious Institute of Poliomyelitis and Viral Encephalitis. He became part of the team that introduced the Sabin polio vaccine in the Soviet Union; his subsequent work at the institute reflected a variety of research interests, among them the response of tumor tissues to lethal viral infections and the biology and pathology of monkeys.

Tsypkin had always been fervent about literature, had always written a little for himself, both prose and poetry. In his early twenties, when he was nearing the completion of his medical studies, he considered quitting medicine in order to study literature, with the idea of devoting himself entirely to writing. Riven by the nineteenth-century Russian soul questions (how to live without faith? without God?), he had idolized Tolstoy, who eventually was replaced by Dostoyevsky. Tsypkin also had cine-loves: Antonioni, for example, but not Tarkovsky. In the early 1960s he had thought about enrolling in night classes at the Institute of Cinematography to become a film director, but the necessity of supporting his family, he said later, made him pull back.

It was also in the early 1960s that Tsypkin began a more committed spate of writing: poems that were strongly influenced by Tsvetayeva and Pasternak; their photographs hung above his small work table. In September 1965 he decided to chance showing some of his lyrics to Andrei Sinyavsky, but Sinyavsky was arrested a few days before their appointment. Tsypkin and Sinyavsky, who were virtually the same age, were never to meet, and Tsypkin became even more cautious. ("My father," says Mikhail Tsypkin, "was not inclined to talk or even to think much about politics. In our family, it was assumed without discussion that the Soviet regime was Evil incarnate.") After several unsuccessful attempts to publish some of his poems, Tsypkin stopped writing for a while. Much of his time was devoted to finishing "A Study of the Morphological and Biological Properties of Cell Cultures of Trypsinized Tissues," his dissertation for a doctor of science degree. (His earlier dissertation, for a Ph.D., was on growth rates of brain tumors that had been subjected to repeated surgeries.) After the successful defense of his second dissertation, in 1969, Tsypkin received an increase in salary, which freed him from moonlighting as a part-time pathologist in a small hospital. Already in his forties, he began writing again—not poetry but prose.

In the thirteen years he had left to live, Tsypkin created a small body of work of ever larger reach and complexity. After a handful of short sketches came longer, more plotted stories, two autobiographical novellas, *The Bridge Across the Neroch* and *Norartakir*, and then his last and longest work of fiction, *Summer in Baden-Baden*, a kind of dream novel, in which the dreamer, who is Tsypkin himself, conjures up his own life and that of Dostoyevsky in a streaming, passionate narration. Writing was engorging, isolating. "Monday through Friday," relates Mikhail Tsypkin, "my father left at a quarter to eight sharp for his work at the Institute of Poliomyelitis and Viral Encephalitis, which was situated in a distant suburb of Moscow, not far from the Vnukovo airport. He came back home at 6 p.m., had dinner, took a short nap, and sat down to write—if not his prose, then his medical research papers. Before going to bed, at 10 p.m., he sometimes took a walk. He usually spent his weekends writing as well. My father craved every opportunity to write, but writing was difficult, painful. He agonized over each word and endlessly corrected his hand-written manuscripts. Once finished with editing, he typed his prose on an ancient, shiny German typewriter, an Erika— Second World War loot that an uncle gave him in 1949. And in that form his writings remained. He did not send his manuscripts to publishers, and did not want to circulate his prose in samizdat because he was afraid of problems with the KGB and of losing his job." Writing without hope or prospect of being published—what resources of faith in literature does that imply? Tsypkin's readership was never much larger than his wife, his son, and a couple of his son's Moscow University classmates. He had no real friends in any of the Moscow literary worlds.

There was one literary personage in Tsypkin's immediate family, his mother's younger sister, the literary critic Lydia Polyak, and readers of *Summer in Baden-Baden* make her glancing acquaintance on the very first page. Aboard a train bound for Leningrad, the narrator opens a book, a precious book whose binding and decorative bookmark are lovingly described before we learn that it is the *Diary* of Dostoyevsky's second wife, Anna Grigoryevna Dostoyevsky, and that this copy, flimsy and almost falling apart when it came into Tsypkin's hands, belongs to an unnamed aunt who can only be Lydia Polyak. Since, Tsypkin writes, "in my heart of hearts I had no intention of returning the book borrowed from my aunt who possessed a large library," he has had it trimmed and rebound.

According to Mikhail Tsypkin, several of his father's stories contain a cranky reference to Polyak. A well-connected member of the Moscow intelligentsia for half a century, she held a research position at the Gorky Institute of World Literature since the 1930s, and even when she was fired from her teaching post at Moscow University during the anti-Semitic purges of the early 1950s, she managed to keep her position at the institute, where Sinyavsky eventually became a junior colleague of hers. Although it was she who arranged the aborted meeting with Sinyavsky, Polyak apparently disapproved of her nephew's writings and condescended to him, for which he never forgave her.

In 1977 Tsypkin's son and daughter-in-law decided to apply for exit visas. Natalya Michnikova, fearing that her employment, for which a security clearance was needed, would prejudice her son's chances, resigned from her job in the division of the State Committee for Material and Technical Supplies (GOSSNAB) that allocated heavy road-building and construction equipment to practically all sectors of the Soviet economy, including the military. The visas were granted, and Mikhail and Elena Tsypkin left for the United States. As soon as the KGB relayed this information to Sergei Drozdov, the director of the Institute for Poliomyelitis and Viral Encephalitis, Tsypkin was demoted to junior researcher—a position for someone without an advanced degree (he had two) and his starting rank of more than twenty years earlier. His salary, now the couple's only source of income, was cut by seventy-five percent. He continued to go to the institute every day but was excluded from laboratory research, which was always conducted by teams; not one of his colleagues was willing to work with Tsypkin, for fear of being tainted by contact with an "undesirable element." There would have been no point in seeking a research position elsewhere, since in every job application he would have had to declare that his son had emigrated.

In June 1979 Tsypkin, his wife, and his mother applied for exit visas. They then waited for almost two years. In April 1981 they were informed that their requests were "inexpedient" and had been denied. (Emigration from the USSR virtually stopped in 1980, when relations with the United States deteriorated as a result of the Soviet invasion of Afghanistan; it became obvious that, for the time being, no favors from Washington would be forthcoming in exchange for permitting Soviet Jews to leave.) It was during this period that Tsypkin wrote most of *Summer in Baden-Baden*.

He started the book in 1977 and completed it in 1980. The writing was preceded by years of preparation: consulting archives and photographing places associated with Dostoyevsky's life as well as those frequented by Dostoyevsky's characters during the seasons and at the times of day mentioned in the novels. (Tsypkin was a dedicated amateur photographer and had owned a camera since the early 1950s.) After finishing *Summer in Baden-Baden*, he presented an album of these photographs to the Dostoyevsky museum in Leningrad.

However inconceivable it was that *Summer in Baden-Baden* could be published in Russia, there was still the option of publishing it abroad, as the best writers were then doing with their work. Tsypkin decided to attempt just this and asked Azary Messerer, a journalist friend who had received permission to leave in early 1981, to smuggle a copy of the manuscript and some of the photographs out of the Soviet Union. Messerer was able to arrange this through the good offices of two American friends, a married couple, who were Moscow-based correspondents for UPI.

At the end of September 1981 Tsypkin, his wife, and his mother reapplied for exit visas. On October 19, Vera Polyak died at the age of eighty-six. The refusal of all three visa applications came a week later; this time, the decision had taken less than a month.

In early March 1982 Tsypkin went to see the head of the Moscow visa office, who told him, "Doctor, you will never be allowed to emigrate." On Monday, March 15, Sergei Drozdov informed Tsypkin that he would no longer be kept on at the institute. The same day Mikhail Tsypkin, who was in graduate school at Harvard, called Moscow to announce that on Saturday his father had finally become a published writer. Azary Messerer had succeeded in placing *Summer in Baden-Baden* with a Russian-émigré weekly in New York, *Novaya Gazeta*, which would be serializing the novel. The first installment, illustrated by some of Tsypkin's photographs, had appeared on March 13.

Early on Saturday, March 20, his fifty-sixth birthday, Tsypkin sat down at his desk to continue work on the translation of a medical text from English into Russian—translating being one of the few possibilities of eking out a living open to refuseniks (Soviet citizens, usually Jews, who had been denied exit visas and fired from their jobs). He suddenly felt unwell (it was a heart attack), lay down, called out to his wife, and died. He had been a published author of fiction for exactly seven days.

.

For Tsypkin, it was a matter of honor that everything of a factual nature in *Summer in Baden-Baden* be true to the story and the circumstances of the real lives it evokes. This is not, like J. M. Coetzee's wonderful *The Master of Petersburg*, a Dostoyevsky fantasy. Neither is it a docu-novel, although Tsypkin was obsessed with getting everything "right." (In his son's words, he was, in all matters, "very systematic.") It is possible that Tsypkin imagined that if *Summer in Baden-Baden* were ever published as a book, it should include some of the photographs he had taken, thereby anticipating the signature effect of the work of W. G. Sebald, who, by seeding his books with photographs, infused the plainest idea of verisimilitude with enigma and pathos.

What kind of a book is *Summer in Baden-Baden*? From the start, it proposes a double narrative. It is wintertime, late December, no date given: a species of "now." The narrator is on a train going to Leningrad (former and future St. Petersburg). And it is mid-April 1867. The newly married Dostoyevskys, Fyodor ("Fedya") and his young wife, Anna Grigoryevna, have left St. Petersburg and are on their way to Dresden. The account of the Dostoyevskys' travels—for they will be mostly abroad in Tsypkin's novel, and not only in Baden-Baden—has been scrupulously researched. The passages where the narrator—Tsypkin—describes his own doings are wholly autobiographical. Since imagination and fact are easily contrasted, we tend to draw genre lessons from this and segregate invented stories (fiction) from real-life narratives (chronicle and autobiography). That's one convention—ours. In Japanese literature the so-called I-novel (*shishōsetsu*), a narrative that is essentially autobiographical but contains invented episodes, is a dominant novel form.

In *Summer in Baden-Baden* several "real" worlds are evoked, described, re-created in a hallucinatory rush of associations. The originality of Tsypkin's novel lies in the way it *moves*, from the displacements of the never-to-be-named narrator, embarked on his journey through the bleak contemporary Soviet landscape, to the life of the peripatetic Dostoyevskys. In the cultural ruin that is the present, the feverish past shines through. Tsypkin is traveling *into* Fedya's and Anna's souls and bodies, as he travels *to* Leningrad. There are prodigious, uncanny acts of empathy.

Tsypkin will stay in Leningrad for a few days: it is a Dostoyevsky pilgrimage (surely not the first), a solitary one (no doubt as usual), that will end in a visit to the house where Dostoyevsky died. The Dostoyevskys are just beginning their impecunious travels; they will remain in Western Europe for four years. (It is worth recalling that the author of *Summer in Baden-Baden* was never allowed outside the Soviet Union.) Dresden, Baden-Baden, Basel, Frankfurt, Paris—their lot is to be constantly agitated by the confusions and humiliations of cramping financial misery, while having to negotiate with a chorus of presumptuous foreigners (porters, coachmen, landladies, waiters, shopkeepers, pawnbrokers, croupiers), and by gusts of whim and of volatile emotions of many kinds. The gambling fever. The moral fevers. The fever of illness. The sensual fevers. The fever of jealousy. The penitential fevers. The fear . . .

The principal intensity depicted in Tsypkin's fictional re-creation of Dostoyevsky's life is not gambling, not writing, not Christing. It is the searing, generous absoluteness (which is not to pronounce on the satisfactoriness) of conjugal love. Who will forget the image of the couple's lovemaking as swimming? Anna's all-forgiving but always dignified love for Fedya rhymes with the love of literature's disciple, Tsypkin, for Dostoyevsky.

Nothing is invented. Everything is invented. The framing action is the trip the narrator is making to the sites of Dostoyevsky's life and novels, part of the preparation (as we come to realize) for the book we hold in our hands. *Summer in Baden-Baden* belongs to a rare and exquisitely ambitious subgenre of the novel: a retelling of the life of a real person of accomplishment from another era, it interweaves this story with a story in the present, the novelist mulling over, trying to gain deeper entry into, the inner life of someone whose destiny it was to have become not only historical but monumental. (Another example, and one of the glories of twentieth-century Italian literature, is *Artemisia* by Anna Banti.)

Tsypkin leaves Moscow on the first page and two-thirds of the way through the book arrives at the Moscow Station in Leningrad. Although aware that somewhere near the station is the "ordinary, grey Petersburg dwelling-house" where Dostoyevsky spent the last years of his life, he walks onward with his suitcase in the icy nocturnal gloom, crossing the Nevsky Prospect to pass by other places associated with Dostoyevsky's last years, then turns up where he always stays in Leningrad, a portion of a dilapidated communal apartment occupied by a tenderly described intimate of his mother, who welcomes him, feeds him, makes up a broken sofa for him to sleep on, and asks him, as she always does, "Are you still as keen on

Dostoyevsky?" When she goes to bed, Tsypkin sinks into a volume plucked at random out of the prerevolutionary edition of Dostoyevsky's collected works in her bookcase, *Diary of a Writer*, and falls asleep musing about the mystery of Dostoyevsky's anti-Semitism.

After a morning spent chatting with his affectionate old friend, and hearing more stories of the horrors endured during the Leningrad Blockade, Tsypkin sets off—the short winter day is already darkening—to roam about the city, "taking photographs of the Raskolnikov House or the Old Money-lender's House or Sonechka's House or buildings where their author had lived during the darkest and most clandestine period of his life in the years immediately following his return from exile." Walking on, "led by a kind of instinct," Tsypkin manages to reach "exactly the right spot"—"my heart was pounding with joy and some other vaguely sensed feeling"—opposite the four-story corner building where Dostoyevsky died, now the Dostoyevsky museum; and the description of the visit ("An almost churchlike silence reigned in the museum") segues into a narrative of a dying that is worthy of Tolstoy. It is through the prism of Anna's excruciating grief that Tsypkin re-creates the long deathbed hours in this book about love, married love and the love of literature—loves that are in no way linked or compared, but each given its due, each contributing its infusing fire.

·

Loving Dostoyevsky, what is one to do—what is a Jew to do—with the knowledge that he hated Jews? How to explain the vicious anti-Semitism of "a man so sensitive in his novels to the suffering of others, this jealous defender of the insulted and injured"? And how to understand "this special attraction which Dostoyevsky seems to possess for Jews"?

The most intellectually powerful of the earlier Jewish Dostoyevsky-lovers is Leonid Grossman (1888–1965), who heads a long list of such figures cited by Tsypkin. Grossman is an important source for Tsypkin's reimagining of Dostoyevsky's life, and one of the books mentioned at the beginning of *Summer in Baden-Baden* is the product of Grossman's scholarly labors. It was he who edited the first selection of Anna Dostoyevsky's *Reminiscences*, which was published in 1925, seven years after her death. Tsypkin speculates that the absence of "loathsome little Jews" and other such expectable phrases in the memoirs of Dostoyevsky's widow may be explained by the fact that she wrote them, on the eve of the Revolution, after she had made Grossman's acquaintance.

Tsypkin must have known Grossman's many influential essays on Dostoyevsky, such as *Balzac and Dostoyevsky* (1914) and *Dostoyevsky's Library* (1919). He may have come across Grossman's novel, *Roulettenburg* (1932), a gloss on Dostoyevsky's novella about the gambling passion. (*Roulettenburg* was the original title of *The Gambler*.) But he couldn't have read Grossman's *Confession of a Jew* (1924), which had gone completely out of circulation. *Confession of a Jew* is an account of the life of the most enthralling and pathetic of the Jewish Dostoyevskyists, Arkady Uri Kovner (1842–1909), brought up in the Vilna ghetto, with whom Dostoyevsky entered an epistolary relationship. A reckless autodidact, Kovner had fallen under the writer's spell and was inspired by reading *Crime and Punishment* to commit a theft to succor an ailing impoverished young woman with whom he was in love. In 1877, from his cell in a Moscow jail, before being transported to serve a sentence of four years of hard labor in Siberia, Kovner wrote to Dostoyevsky to challenge him on the matter of his antipathy to Jews. (That was the first letter; the second was about the immortality of the soul.)

In the end, there is no resolution of the anguishing subject of Dostoyevsky's anti-Semitism, a theme that comes surging into *Summer in Baden-Baden* once Tsypkin reaches Leningrad. It seemed, he writes, "strange to the point of implausibility . . . that this man should not have come up with even a single word in the defense or justification of a people persecuted over several thousand years . . . and he did not even refer to the Jews as a people, but as a tribe . . . and to this tribe I belonged and the many friends and acquaintances of mine with whom I had discussed the subtlest problems of Russian literature." Yet this hasn't kept Jews from loving Dostoyevsky. How to explain that?

Tsypkin has no better explanation than the fervor of Jews for the greatness of Russian literature—which might remind us that the German worship of Goethe and Schiller was in large part a Jewish affair, right up to the time Germany started murdering its Jews. Loving Dostoyevsky means loving literature.

·

A crash course on all the great themes of Russian literature, *Summer in Baden-Baden* is unified by the ingenuity and velocity of its language, which moves boldly, seductively, between first and third person—the doings, memories, musings of the narrator ("I") and the Dostoyevsky scenes ("he," "they," "she")—and between past and present. But this is not a unitary present (of the narrator Tsypkin on his Dostoyevsky pilgrimage), any more than it is a unitary past (the Dostoyevskys from 1867 to 1881, the year of Dostoyevsky's death). Dostoyevsky, in the past, submits to the undertow of remembered scenes, passions from earlier moments in his life; the narrator, in the present, summons up memories of his past.

Each paragraph indent begins a long, long sentence whose connectives are "and" (many of these) and "but" (several) and "although" and "and so" and "whereas" and "just as" and "because" and "as if," along with many dashes, and there is a full stop only when the paragraph ends. In the course of these ardently protracted paragraph-sentences, the river of feeling gathers up and sweeps along the narrative of Dostoyevsky's life and of Tsypkin's: a sentence that starts with Fedya and Anna in Dresden might flash back to Dostoyevsky's convict years or to an earlier bout of gambling mania linked to his romance with Polina Suslova, then thread onto this a memory from the narrator's medical-student days and a rumination on some lines by Pushkin.

Tsypkin's sentences call to mind José Saramago's run-on sentences, which fold dialogue into description and description into dialogue, and are spiked by verbs that refuse to stay consistently in either the past or the present tense. In their incessantness, Tsypkin's sentences have something of the same force and hectic authority as those of Thomas Bernhard. Obviously, Tsypkin could not have known the books of Saramago and Bernhard. He had other models of ecstatic prose in twentieth-century literature. He loved the early (not the late) prose of Pasternak—*Safe Conduct*, not *Doctor Zhivago*. He loved Tsvetayeva. He loved Rilke, in part because Tsvetayeva and Pasternak had loved Rilke; he read very little foreign literature and only in translation. Of what he had read, his greatest passion was

Kafka, whom he discovered by way of a volume of stories published in the Soviet Union in the mid-1960s. The amazing Tsypkin sentence was entirely his own invention.

Reminiscing about his father, Tsypkin's son describes him as obsessed by detail and compulsively neat. His daughter-in-law, commenting on his choice of medical specialty— pathology—and his decision never to practice as a clinical physician, recalls that "he was very interested in death." Perhaps only an obsessive, death-haunted hypochondriac, such as Tsypkin seems to have been, could have devised a sentence-form that is free in so original a way. His prose is an ideal vehicle for the emotional intensity and abundance of his subject. In a relatively short book, the long sentence bespeaks inclusiveness and associativeness, the passionate agility of a temperament steeped, in most respects, in adamancy.

Besides the account of the incomparable Dostoyevsky, Tsypkin's novel offers an extraordinary mental tour of Russian reality. Taken for granted, if that is not too odd a way of putting it, are the sufferings of the Soviet era, from the Great Terror of 1934–37 to the present of the narrator's quest: the book pulses with them. *Summer in Baden-Baden* is also a spirited and plangent account of Russian literature—the whole arc of Russian literature. Pushkin, Turgenev (there is a scene of fierce confrontation between Dostoyevsky and Turgenev), and the great figures of twentieth-century literature and ethical struggle—Tsvetayeva, Solzhenitsyn, Sakharov, and Bonner—also enter, are poured into the narration.

One emerges from reading *Summer in Baden-Baden* purged, shaken, fortified, breathing a little deeper, grateful to literature for what it can harbor and exemplify. Leonid Tsypkin did not write a long book. But he made a great journey.

A Double Destiny

On *Anna Banti's* Artemisia

"Non piangere." Don't cry. These are the opening words of
Anna Banti's novel *Artemisia*. Who is talking? And when? The
first-person voice—that of the author—writes "this August
day," omitting both the date and the year, but these are not hard
to fill in. August 4, 1944; late in the Second World War—
this is when Banti's novel, whose protagonist is the seventeenth-
century Italian painter Artemisia Gentileschi, begins. Nazi
Germany's occupation of Florence, following the collapse of
the Mussolini government, has taken its appalling, final turn. At
four o'clock that morning the Germans, who had begun evacu-
ating the city, detonated the mines they had set along the Arno,
managing to blow up all the venerable bridges except the Ponte
Vecchio and to wreck many houses on or near the river, among
them the house on the Borgo San Jacopo where Banti lived,
under the ruins of which lay the manuscript of her new novel,
nearly completed, about Artemisia Gentileschi.

"Non piangere." Don't cry. Who is talking? And where? It's the author, still in her nightgown (as in a dream, she writes), sitting on a gravel path in the Boboli Gardens—on the promontory on the south side of the Arno—sobbing, telling herself not to cry, and finally ceasing to cry, stunned by the ever sharper realization of what was destroyed in the havoc of a few hours before. Florence's *centro storico* is still burning. There is fighting, gunfire. (It will be another seven days before the whole city is liberated by the Allies.) Refugees have clustered higher up, at the Forte di Belvedere, from which she descended a little earlier; here, she writes, there is no one nearby. Soon she will stand and look at the rubble lining the Arno. And a whole day will pass. After the "white troubled dawn" in the Boboli Gardens of the first lines of the novel, it will be noon (there's a reference to the South African soldiers who entered the city six hours earlier), and Banti will have taken refuge below in the Palatine gallery of the Palazzo Pitti, and then dusk, when she will be once more at the Forte di Belvedere (where, she says, people are risking being machine-gunned to lie out on the grass), and from that commanding view she will continue grieving for Florence and the death all around her, and for the manuscript that exists now only in her fragile memory.

"Non piangere." Don't cry. Who is talking to whom? It is the stricken author talking to herself, telling herself to be brave. But she is also addressing the heroine of her novel, "my companion from three centuries ago," who had lived again on the pages in which Banti had told her story. And as she mourns, images of Artemisia surge through Banti's mind, first of "a disillusioned and despairing Artemisia," middle-aged, in Naples, not long before her death, then of Artemisia as a child in Rome, ten years old, "her delicate features expressing pride and ill-treatment." Mocking the loss of the manuscript, "the images continue to flow with a mechanical, ironical ease, secreted by this shattered world." *Artemisia* is lost, but Artemisia, her lamenting phantom presence, is everywhere, irrepressible. Soon—Artemisia's distress, and Banti's, are too keen—the anguished first-person voice of the author makes way for the voice of Artemisia, and then gives itself permission to become intermittently, then for longer stretches, the third-person voice that narrates the painter's life.

For what the reader holds is, of course, the novel written—written again—in the following three years and published in late 1947, when Anna Banti (the pen name of Lucia Lopresti) was fifty-two years old. Although she was to publish sixteen works of fiction and autobiographical prose before her death at the age of ninety, in 1985, this—her second novel—is the one that assures her a place in world literature.

A phoenix of a book, written out of the ashes of another book, the novel is a tribute to bitterness and to tenacity—that of the bereft little girl of the early 1600s who will, against all odds, become a renowned painter, that of the bereaved author who will write a novel that is surely more original than the one consumed in the fires of war. Loss has made the author free to enter the book, talking to herself and to Artemisia. ("Don't cry.") Artemisia has become even more dear to the author, whose feeling has deepened, become almost amorous. Artemisia is the elusive beloved who, because of the loss of the manuscript, is now more intensely present in the author's mind and more exigent than ever. It is a love relationship yet to be fully described, that between the author, alternately tender and querulous, and the quarry, the victim, the tyrant whose attention and complicity she desires.

Never has the passion of novelist for protagonist been so intently formulated. Like Virginia Woolf's *Orlando, Artemisia* is a kind of dance with its protagonist: through it course all the relations that the author can devise with the fascinating woman whose biographer she has decided to be. The lost novel has been recast as a novel about a haunting. Nothing so crude as an identification: Anna Banti does not find herself in Artemisia Gentileschi—any more, or less, than Woolf thinks that she is Orlando. On the contrary, Artemisia is forever and supremely someone else. And the novelist is her thrall—her amanuensis. Sometimes Artemisia is coquettishly inaccessible. ("In order to further reproach me and make me regret her loss, she lowers her eyelids, as though to let me know that she is thinking about something and that she will never tell me what it is.") Other times she is yielding, seductive. ("Now it is for my benefit alone that Artemisia recites her lesson; she wants to prove to me that she believes everything that I invented . . .") The book is a testament, dictated by Artemisia. But also a tale, propelled by whim and filled out with figments of the author's imagination, not at all at Artemisia's behest, though she may waive her objections. Banti asks and receives Artemisia's permission to tell. She runs up against Artemisia's reluctance to admit the author to her thoughts. The game of concealment is mutual: "We are playing a chasing game, Artemisia and I."

At one moment Banti claims she no longer cares for the book that was nearly finished: "Even if I saw the lost manuscript with all its marks, its blotches, lying beside me on the grass that still resounds with the noise of the cannon, I couldn't be bothered to read a line of it." But that is mere bravado. Artemisia lingers, importunate, in Banti's mind. Why should she be dismissed? After all, "a prisoner needs to amuse himself somehow, and I have very few playthings left, only a doll that I can dress and undress; particularly undress . . . If Artemisia were still a ghost and not a weighty, strange name, she would shudder at my disrespectful digressions."

An author who may be described as a lover of sorts is, inevitably, one who insists on being there—brooding, interrupting, prowling about in her book. Relentlessly dialogical (it is in the nature of the language of love to be dialogical), the novel offers an impassioned mix of first- and third-person voices. The "I" usually belongs to Banti but can be, on poignant narrative occasions, that of Artemisia herself. The third-person voice offers classically detached, omniscient narration or, much of the time, that warmer variant called free indirect discourse, which clings so closely to the thoughts of a character that it amounts to a transposed or disguised first person. The author, with her fervent avowals and nervous probing of what can and cannot be said about Artemisia, on Artemisia's behalf, is never far away.

The novel is a conversation that the author is having with Artemisia—Banti speaks, daringly, of feeling bound to the novel by "our conversations"—but other claims are evoked, too, as if to affirm a cooler relation with her character (of whom, Banti has already declared in the preface, she is "perhaps too fond"). Their bond resembles "a sort of contract legally drawn up between lawyer and client, and which I must honor." Or, Banti proposes, Artemisia "is a creditor, a stubborn, scrupulous conscience to which I grow accustomed as to sleeping on the ground." All this to explain—or further complicate—the truth that, as Banti realizes, she "will never be able to be free of Artemisia again."

Banti's presence in the narrative is at the heart—is the heart—of the novel. In another passage, Banti is imagining the notorious drama of Artemisia's adolescence, when she was already an artist of startlingly large accomplishment: her rape in 1611 by a painter colleague of her eminent father; the decision to make the rape public and seek justice; the trial, in 1612, in which the juvenile plaintiff was subjected to torture to determine if she was telling the truth; Artemisia's vindication (which did not lessen the scandal), after which her often absent father left Rome for Florence, taking his disgraced daughter with him. And now it is autumn 1944, in Florence, and Banti describes herself as "dragging Artemisia on a walk through the Boboli Gardens, battered and deserted after the departure of the refugees; and I compel her to move along with the remaining few, the unhappy proprietors of this large, polluted area, there to meet prostitutes and rough soldiers." In Banti's ingenious dramatizing of an author's freedom to imagine, to re-create, to invent—traditional prerogatives that apply no less to the novels called "historical," informed by documents—Artemisia has become the ward of a tormented, peremptory author, who claims the right to drag a re-created real person about, impose new feelings on her, even change her appearance. At one moment, Banti notes, Artemisia has "become so docile that even the color of her hair changes, becomes almost black, and her complexion olive, such as I imagined her when I first read the accounts of her trial in the mold-colored documents. I close my eyes and for the first time use 'tu' to her."

Roaming the story as a yearning conjurer of her protagonist, Banti remains in her own time. It is Artemisia who becomes a time-traveler, a visitor, a phantom so real she can be measured even physically in the author's consciousness. Thus Artemisia's narration of her rape is as told to the author, and when the pitiful story breaks off, Banti says, "she rests her head on my shoulder, it weighs no more than a sparrow." Indeed, the account of the rape, early in the novel and startling in its brevity, is entirely enclosed in the dialogical exchange with Banti.

Artemisia's spectral incursions into Banti's present load every move in the advancing narration of the painter's life with emotional urgency, a claim for a preternatural degree of intimacy with the inaccessible past. "Trapped in time and space like an infertile seed, I listen to a stale rustling, the dusty breathing of centuries, our own and Artemisia's combined." There are conventional spasms of discouragement. It is a year later, 1945: "I now admit," she writes, "that it is not possible to recall to life and understand an action that happened three hundred years ago, far less an emotion, and what at the time was sadness or happiness." More arrestingly, Banti asks herself whether the new blow of reality—the war and its devastations—has not outpaced the concerns of the novel and altered the terms in which it can be written. "The rhythm of her story had its own moral and meaning which perhaps have collapsed as the result of my recent experiences. A moral and a meaning with which I trifle. Artemisia will have to be satisfied with what follows next."

And then the novel returns to the painter's—the woman's—story.

.

Today the only woman who is a member of the incomparable succession of European Old Masters, Artemisia Gentileschi was not a canonical painter when Banti decided to make her the principal character in a novel. Still, this particular life might seem an obvious subject for this author. Banti's first decade of writing, the 1920s, was devoted to art history, and she returned occasionally to publishing monographs about painters (Lorenzo Lotto, Fra Angelico, Velázquez, Monet) during the period, the 1950s and 1960s, when she was most prolific as a fiction writer. Nearly all her stories and novels had female protagonists—women of exceptional spirit, solitary women (who may be the wives of powerful men), indignant women; the author's indignation must be inferred from what the austere, elegant third-person narrative voice leaves unsaid. The recurrent use of such characters suggests Banti's mixed feelings about her own ambitions and achievements. It appears that in the 1930s she dreamed of becoming a film director, something impossible in fascist Italy, and only then turned to writing fiction. (Her first work was a short story published in a literary magazine in 1934, for which she adopted the pseudonym that she used from then on.) As she was to say at the end of her long life, her predilection was for stories of women, "wise in their own way," who become "aware that good has been defeated" and that their destiny is "an unhappy mediocrity"—not stories of successful perseverance in an artistic vocation.

The novel about Artemisia Gentileschi, written in a relentlessly emotional voice, is the great exception: an account of the triumph of an immensely gifted woman at a time when an independent career in the arts was a nearly unthinkable option for a woman.

Aptly enough, the name Artemisia is associated with female assertiveness, with women doing well what men do. In Greek mythology, Artemis—Artemisia means "follower of Artemis"—is the goddess of the hunt. In history— Herodotus' great *History*, which recounts the attempt of the Persian empire to conquer the tiny, independent Greek city-states on the northwest edge of Xerxes' vast domains—it is the name of a queen and a military leader: Artemisia, Queen of Halicarnassus, a Greek city in Ionia, who joined the Persians and was put in command by Xerxes of five of his ships.

As vocations go, a Greek queen commanding a Persian naval squadron is only slightly more improbable than a seventeenth-century Italian woman becoming a much-sought-after professional painter of large narrative compositions with biblical or classical subjects—many of which depict women's rage and women's victimization. Women killing men—Judith hacking away at Holofernes, Jael dispatching Sisera. And women killing themselves—Cleopatra, Lucrezia. Women vulnerable or humiliated or suing for mercy—Susanna and the Elders, the Penitent Magdalene, Esther before Ahasuerus. All subjects that suggest the torments of Artemisia herself, who had already done something heroic, virtually unheard of: denouncing a rapist in a court and demanding his conviction. (Banti imagines "the young Artemisia desperate to be justified, to be avenged, to be in command.") Her heroism, her ambition are intimately connected with her disgrace; she is, as it were, liberated by disgrace, by scandal—the scandal of a rape made public by the victim herself (as the martial talents of Herodotus' Artemisia may be imagined to have been liberated by the scandal of the queen's defection to the enemy side).

Banti retells Artemisia's decision: "So I said, I'll go on my own; I thought then that after my disgrace I at least had the right to be as free as a man." For a woman to be free, free as a man, means choices—sacrifices—sufferings that a man may choose but is not obliged to incur. In Banti's account, what is central to Artemisia's life is not the rape; not the marriage with an obscure young man that her father imposed on her once the verdict was brought against the rapist; nor the four children (three of whom died) she bore her husband. It is her solitude, the inexorable result of her commitment to her art. It is her loneliness, for in Banti's understanding, the principal relation in Artemisia's life is to someone whom she loves unconditionally, reverently, and who does not love her: her father, Orazio Gentileschi, master painter and friend of Caravaggio. (On the art history map both father and daughter figure as Baroque painters who operated in the large wake of Caravaggism.) It was he who trained his precocious daughter as well as her three younger brothers, who proved run-of-the-mill talents. But he was an infrequent presence in Artemisia's life and spent his last twenty years in Genoa, in Paris, and finally in England, one of a circle of painters that included Anthony Van Dyck at the court of Charles I, the most important collector of paintings of the age. As the principal relation of Artemisia's life is to this severe, rejecting father, the most amply and thrillingly narrated event in the novel is the journey Artemisia makes alone, by sea and overland, from Naples (via Leghorn, Genoa, Paris, and Calais) to London, when she is suddenly summoned by Orazio, now seventy-four, to join him as a fellow painter at the English court.

While heroic in that she defies the norms of her sex (and puts aside womanly needs that would make her weak) in order to become an artist, Artemisia is a familiar feminine type. Her life and character are organized by her fear of and subservience to her opaque, masterful father. There is no mother in Artemisia's life. The missing maternal presence is supplied by Banti—an author in search of her character, instead of the reverse, Pirandellian, quest—as if somehow Artemisia's pain, Artemisia's sorrows, could be alleviated by the gift of sympathy that would come when an Italian writer born in 1895 would bring back to life the Italian painter born in the 1590s and would really understand her.*

---

* Trained as an art historian, Banti was as respectful of the available sources as she could be, and the novel conveys a brilliantly researched sense of the period. The changes Banti made in the character or life were in the name of her uniquely possessive relation to Artemisia (child, beloved, sorrowsister, familiar), and are avowed; they are part of the emotional play of the novel. But the writer's deliberate choice to alter known facts in a novel based on a real historical personage must be distinguished from imperfect knowledge. Thus 1598, the year Banti gives in the prefatory "Note to the Reader" for Artemisia's birth, was the date accepted then. Only some twenty years after the publication of Banti's novel was a birth certificate discovered that establishes that Artemisia Gentileschi was born in 1593.

With Banti's date the Artemisia who was raped was thirteen. And she would have been twelve when she executed her first major painting, *Susanna and the Elders,* signed and dated 1610. The rape, and Artemisia's willingness to press charges against her rapist and undergo torture at the trial to "prove" her veracity—not to mention the ability to produce such a mature, brilliant painting—make for a rather different, though no less astonishing, story now that we know she was in her late teens.

Toward the end of the novel, when Artemisia is alone, abandoned, in England, where her father has just died—the year is 1638—there is another intersection of the centuries, for it is also 1939, and Banti, on a trip to England and no doubt thinking of the book she is going to write or has already begun, is looking—without success—for Orazio's grave. And then the novel follows Artemisia as she travels back to Naples, her thoughts only of death. Mourning her father, preparing for her own death in an overturned carriage or in a shipwreck or at the hands of brigands (there are many other versions of this fearsome imminent death), Artemisia does in fact surmount the journey's perils and hardships and succeeds in breaking free of her death-bound despair and even of her "cruel, closed century" by accepting her own physical needs— hunger, thirst, sleep—and a spectral consolation, "an indefinable presentiment of some benevolent age, of some kindred spirit who alone would know how to weep for her."

A kindred spirit? In what sense? There is the sympathy extended to her within the novel by Banti—a declared bond of sorrow that connects author and protagonist; a healing act of solidarity as the author encounters those sorrowful feelings in herself as well as in Artemisia. But there is no reflection in the novel of another bond existing between author and protagonist—their enslavement by admiration, justified admiration, of a commanding, important male mentor—although the twentieth-century author of *Artemisia* was just as identified with a famous man in the same profession as the seventeenth-century painter was.

Indeed, Artemisia's worship of her father seems a transposition of Anna Banti's reverence for her husband, Italy's pre-eminent twentieth-century critic, art historian, and cultural arbiter, Roberto Longhi (1890–1970). It was Longhi who, among his many potent reassessments, launched the modern rediscovery of the Gentileschis, father and daughter, as important painters in an article published in 1916. Banti had been Longhi's student when the prodigious young scholar taught art history at a *liceo* in Rome; she was twenty-nine and he was thirty-four, and had been teaching for two years at the University of Rome, when they married. His collaborator in all his activities, a lecturer and writer on art and then an editor and frequent contributor to *Paragone*, the influential magazine of the visual arts and literature that Longhi founded in 1950, Banti remained in her husband's shadow, in his intellectual service, throughout their nearly half-century of marriage— even as her own reputation as a writer grew. (*Artemisia* is dedicated to Longhi.)

It is always more defining for a female artist than for a male artist to have a male mentor. Thus Anna Banti is never mentioned without explaining that she was the wife of Roberto Longhi (the reverse is not true)—just as Artemisia Gentileschi is always introduced as the daughter of the great Orazio Gentileschi. And this is how Banti, like Artemisia, saw herself.

To be sure, all this lies outside what is avowed in *Artemisia*. It was avowable at the end. Banti's last book, published in 1981, eleven years after Longhi's death, when she was eighty-six, is her most directly autobiographical novel. Translated under the title *A Piercing Cry*—for the Italian *Un grido lacerante*—it is a naked book, a book of widow's suffering, of clamorous self-deprecation. How bereft and without value she felt since the death of *il Maestro*—which is how Banti's alter ego narrator, Agnese, refers to her magisterial husband throughout the novel. (The English translation has her call him, somewhat less imposingly, "the Professor.") The novel gives a wrenchingly insecure account of her work as a writer of fiction, replete with doubts about whether it had been worthwhile to write fiction at all. She should have remained a scholar of art history and a literary critic, even if nothing she wrote could live up to Longhi's near-prophetic standards of scholarship and the renovation of taste. Her ventures into fiction, her "stories of proud and indignant women," were bound to be viewed with condescension, as a dereliction of duty. Hence the pseudonym: "If she failed, her fiasco would not involve anyone. This name, somewhat dull and lacking grace, was all she owned . . . When her books began to be published (and each time she considered them with a genuine skepticism) she realized that they earned a respectful approval, but they were also regarded with suspicion: she was primarily the wife of a prominent man, and she had to pay for the privilege."

The pseudonym is not just a cover, it is a vow of reticence. To write works of fiction, in addition to literary criticism and film reviews, was what distinguished her existence as a writer from Longhi's. In fiction, Banti gives voice to feelings and experiences different from his—those of a woman, and one married to this famous man—and displaces them. Thus the extremely intimate "I" of *Artemisia* resolutely abstains from any autobiographical material. The only relationship Banti declares in the book is with Artemisia. With Artemisia she suffers, from Artemisia she learns: "Through

Artemisia I have come to realize all the forms, all the different ways in which the grief of a violated purity can express itself."

Speaking of Artemisia's pain, she writes: "I had thought, with my pages, to have alleviated it." But Banti, who had to have been aware of the very complex, harsh feelings that went into the making of the novel, cannot help presenting herself as an aggressor against Artemisia, as well as her rescuer. Her novel is a cruel game as well as an act of love, an expiation as well as a deliverance. She interrupts the story to declare: "This awakening of Artemisia is my own awakening. The immunities granted by the war, the extraordinary freedom that everyone felt he was allowed, have ended." What she dared think of as "a joint collaboration, active and shared, the convulsive game of two shipwrecked women who do not want to abandon the hope of being saved," has faded. And Artemisia "has merged once more into the distant light of three centuries ago, a light which she shines full into my face, blinding me."

Discouragement again. And the repeal of discouragement soon after. The novelist has set herself an impossible task. Of course, Banti cannot, by a kind of sympathetic magic across the centuries, heal Artemisia's sufferings or console her for them. But she can, by assuming the full burden of sympathy, console and fortify herself. And the reader—especially the woman reader.

·

Artemisia is hardly the only important novel that testifies to the situation of being haunted, inhabited by the leading character. (Marguerite Yourcenar's *Memoirs of Hadrian* is another.) But this one is, specifically, about a woman of great accomplishment haunted by another woman of great accomplishment. Therefore if for no other reason, Banti's novel has a feminist resonance. But not surprisingly, Banti always repudiated any ascription of feminist feeling or attitudes. In a late letter she admitted to admiring Virginia Woolf—she wrote about her and in 1950 translated *Jacob's Room*—but added that she did not find Woolf "congenial." Feminism, she says of her alter ego in *A Piercing Cry*, is "a word that she hated."

To refuse, vehemently (even scornfully) refuse, a reputation as a feminist was, of course, a common move for the most brilliant and independent women of her generation—Woolf being the glorious exception. Think of Hannah Arendt. Or of Colette, who once declared that women who were so stupid as to want the vote deserved "the whip and the harem." (*La Vagabonde*, her novel-manifesto about a woman choosing her career and a single life over the love of a worthy man and emotional dependence, was translated into Italian by Banti.) Feminism has meant many things; many unnecessary things. It can be defined as a position—about justice and dignity and liberty—to which almost all independent women would adhere if they did not fear the retaliation that accompanies a word with such a sulfurous reputation. Or it can be defined as a position easier to disavow or quarrel with, as it was by Banti (and Arendt and Colette). That version of feminism suggests that there is a war against men, which was anathema to such women; that feminism suggests an avowal of strength—and a denial of the difficulty and the cost for women in being strong (above all, the cost in masculine support and affection); more, it proclaims pride in being a woman, it even affirms the superiority of women—all attitudes that felt alien to the many independent women who were proud of their accomplishments and who knew the sacrifices and the compromises they entailed.

Artemisia is full of affirmations of the pathos of female identity: women's weakness, women's dependence, women's solitariness (should they want to be anything but daughters, wives, and mothers), women's sorrows, women's grief. To be a woman is to be incarcerated, and to struggle against incarceration, and to long for it. "'If only I were not a woman,' that futile lament," Banti's Artemisia reflects. "Far better to ally herself with the sacrificed and imprisoned, participate in their veiled, momentous fate, share their feelings, their plans, their truths; secrets from which the privileged, men, were barred." But, of course, Artemisia's achievement—her genius—banishes her from this home.

Artemisia has had a husband, a decent man, who after some years is no longer at her side. She has had a daughter, who grows up neglected by her mother and eventually ceases to love her. She has chosen to become, to try to become, "a woman who has renounced all tenderness, all claim to feminine virtues"—virtue in a woman means self-abnegation— "in order to dedicate herself solely to painting." *Artemisia* is a tragic reflection on the condition of being a woman and of defying the norms of one's sex—as opposed to the comic, triumphalist, tender fable that is *Orlando.* As an account of exemplary tribulations that follow from being independent, an artist, and a woman, Banti's novel is also exemplary in its despair and its defiance: the merit of Artemisia's choice is never in doubt.

Read only as a feminist novel, which *Artemisia* certainly

is, it confirms what we know (or think we know; or want others to know). But its power as literature is also that of an encounter with what we don't know or fully understand. The feeling of strangeness is a particular effect of that branch of literature tamed by the label "historical fiction." To write well about the past is to write something like fantastic fiction. It is the strangeness of the past, rendered with piercing concreteness, that gives the effect of realism.

As with *Orlando*, the conventional categories—historical novel, biographical novel, fictionalized biography—hardly do justice to *Artemisia*. It offers, among its many pleasures, a headstrong, moving reflection on the presumptions of imaginative literature, at the same time as it celebrates the completeness of the imagination that fulfills itself through painting. Much of the novel's force derives from Banti's knowing appreciation of how the hand, the eye, the mind paint.

Agnese, the autobiographical protagonist of *A Piercing Cry*, calls a novel she has written about Artemisia Gentileschi "the book she loved most." Did she mentally exempt it from her wish that she could destroy all the books of fiction she had published? She doesn't like being thought of as "a woman writer" and is infuriated by philistine women acquaintances who "each claimed to have read at least one of her books (always the same one)." (Undoubtedly it was *Artemisia*.) She writhes under "the accusation of feminism" and allows, as she recalls the stories she had chosen to tell, that it was perhaps "justifiable." She yearns, after having been for so long in the faithful service of "the hypothetical interpretation of history," to make a fresh start. She wishes—but then does not wish—she could write "the modern novel": one "stuffed with an already obsolete present."

Stories that take place in the past are often assumed to be old-fashioned in form and concern. The very fact of being concerned with the past is taken to be an evasion or an escape from the present. But there is nothing retrograde about *Artemisia*, with its intricate, daring exploration of what it is to make up a story based on real people—like the stories of most novels, not just the ones called historical novels. In fact, under the guise of historical or biographical novels—fictional versions of a real person's life—are more than a few of the most original works of fiction written in the twentieth century. In the plangent fullness and uncanny sensual precision of its re-creation of a past world, and in its portrait of the evolution of a heroic consciousness, *Artemisia* belongs with Penelope Fitzgerald's masterpiece, *The Blue Flower*—an account of the life of the poet Novalis. Its obsessive connection with its protagonist, its dialogical or interrogative voices, the double narrative (taking place both in the past and in the present), and the free intermingling of first- and third-person narration give it a family resemblance to Leonid Tsypkin's *Summer in Baden-Baden*—an account of the life of Dostoyevsky. Such books—like *The Memoirs of Hadrian*, they center on arduous physical journeys, which are also journeys of a wounded soul—would be trivialized by calling them historical novels. And, if the term has any use, at the very least one needs to distinguish between novels that assume an absolute, omniscient voice, recounting the past, and those with a dialogical voice, which set a story in the past in order to dwell on its relation to the present—very much a modern project.

Anna Banti did not want to lose her manuscript in the battle for Florence in early August 1944. No writer could welcome such a destiny. But there can be no doubt that what

makes *Artemisia* a great book—and unique in Banti's work—
is this double destiny, of a book lost and re-created. A book
that by being posthumous, rewritten, resurrected, gained
incalculably in emotional reach and moral authority. A
metaphor for literature, perhaps. And a metaphor for reading,
militant reading—which, at its worthiest, is rereading—too.

Unextinguished

The Case for Victor Serge

•

"After all, there is such a thing as truth."

—The Case of Comrade Tulayev

How to explain the obscurity of one of the most compelling of twentieth-century ethical and literary heroes, Victor Serge? How to account for the neglect of *The Case of Comrade Tulayev*, a wonderful novel that has gone on being rediscovered and reforgotten ever since its publication, a year after Serge's death in 1947?

Is it because no country can fully claim him? "A political exile since my birth"—so Serge (real name: Victor Lvovich Kibalchich) described himself. His parents were opponents of tsarist tyranny who had fled Russia in the early 1880s, and Serge was born in 1890 "in Brussels, as it happened, in mid-journey across the world," he relates in his *Memoirs of a Revolutionary*, written in 1942 and 1943 in Mexico City, where, a penurious refugee from Hitler's Europe and Stalin's assassins at large, he spent his last years. Before Mexico, Serge had lived, written, conspired, and propagandized in six countries:

Belgium, in his early youth and again in 1936; France, repeatedly; Spain, in 1917—it was then that he adopted the pen
name of Serge; Russia, the homeland he saw for the first time
in early 1919, at the age of twenty-eight, when he arrived to
join the Bolshevik Revolution; and Germany and Austria in
the mid-1920s, on Comintern business. In each country his
residence was provisional, full of hardship and contention,
threatened. In several, it ended with Serge booted out, ban-
ished, obliged to move on.

Is it because he was not—the familiar model—a writer
engaged intermittently in political partisanship and struggle,
like Silone and Camus and Koestler and Orwell, but a lifelong
activist and agitator? In Belgium he militated in the Young
Socialist movement, a branch of the Second International. In
France he became an anarchist (the so-called individualist
kind) and, for articles in the anarchist weekly he coedited that
expressed a modicum of sympathy for the notorious Bonnot
gang after the bandits' arrest (there was never any question of
Serge's complicity) and his refusal, after his arrest, to turn in-
former, was sentenced to five years of solitary confinement.
In Barcelona following his release from prison, he quickly became disillusioned with the Spanish anarcho-syndicalists for
their reluctance to attempt to seize power. Back in France in
late 1917 he was incarcerated for fifteen months, this time as
(the words of the arrest order) "an undesirable, a defeatist,
and a Bolshevik sympathizer." In Russia he joined the Communist Party, fought in the siege of Petrograd during the civil
war, was commissioned to examine the archives of the tsarist
secret police (and wrote a treatise on state oppression), headed
the administrative staff of the executive committee of the

Third—Communist—International and participated in its first three congresses, and, distressed by the mounting barbarity of governance in the newly consolidated Union of Soviet Socialist Republics, arranged to be sent abroad by the Comintern in 1922 as a propagandist and organizer. (In this time there were more than a few freelance, foreign members of the Comintern, which was, in effect, the Foreign, or World Revolution, Department of the Russian Communist Party.) After the failure of revolution in Berlin and subsequent time spent in Vienna, Serge returned in 1926 to the USSR now ruled by Stalin and officially joined the Left Opposition, Trotsky's coalition, with which he had been allied since 1923: he was expelled from the Party in late 1927 and arrested soon after. All in all, Serge was to endure more than ten years of captivity for his serial revolutionary commitments. There is a problem for writers who exercise another, more strenuous profession full-time.

Is it because—despite all these distractions—he wrote so much? Hyperproductivity is not as well regarded as it used to be, and Serge was unusually productive. His published writings—almost all of which are out of print—include seven novels, two volumes of poetry, a collection of short stories, a late diary, his memoirs, some thirty political and historical books and pamphlets, three political biographies, and hundreds of articles and essays. And there was more: a memoir of the anarchist movement in pre–First World War France, a novel about the Russian Revolution, a short book of poems, and a historical chronicle of year two of the revolution, all confiscated, when Serge was finally allowed to leave the USSR in 1936, as the consequence of his having applied to Glavlit, the literary censor, for an exit permit for his manuscripts—

these have never been recovered—as well as a great deal of safely archived but still unpublished material. If anything, his being prolific has probably counted against him.

Is it because most of what he wrote does not belong to literature? Serge began writing fiction—his first novel, *Men in Prison*—when he was thirty-nine. Behind him lay more than twenty years' worth of works of expert historical assessment and political analysis, and a profusion of brilliant political and cultural journalism. He is commonly remembered, if at all, as a valiant dissident Communist, a clear-eyed, assiduous opponent of Stalin's counterrevolution. (Serge was the first to call the USSR a "totalitarian" state, in a letter he wrote to friends in Paris on the eve of his arrest in Leningrad in February 1933.) No twentieth-century novelist had anything like his firsthand experiences of insurgency, of intimate contact with epochal leaders, of dialogue with founding political intellectuals. He had known Lenin—Serge's wife Liubov Rusakova was Lenin's stenographer in 1921; Serge had translated *State and Revolution* into French and wrote a biography of Lenin soon after his death in January 1924. He was close to Trotsky, although they did not meet again after Trotsky's banishment in 1929; Serge was to translate *The Revolution Betrayed* and other late writings and, in Mexico, where Trotsky had preceded him as a political refugee, collaborate with his widow on a biography. Antonio Gramsci and Georg Lukács were among Serge's interlocutors, with whom he discussed, when they were all living in Vienna in 1924 and 1925, the despotic turn that the revolution had taken almost immediately, under Lenin. In *The Case of Comrade Tulayev*, whose epic subject is the Stalinist state's murder of millions of the Party faithful as well as of most dissidents in the 1930s, Serge writes about a fate he himself most improbably, and just barely, escaped. Serge's novels have been admired principally as testimony; polemic; inspired journalism; fictionalized history. It is easy to underestimate the literary accomplishment of a writer the bulk of whose work is not literary.

Is it because no national literature can entirely claim him? Cosmopolitan by vocation, he was fluent in five languages: French, Russian, German, Spanish, and English. (He spent part of his childhood in England.) In his fiction, he has to be considered a Russian writer, bearing in mind the extraordinary continuity of Russian voices in literature—one whose forebears are Dostoyevsky, the Dostoyevsky of *The House of the Dead* and *The Devils*, and Chekhov, and whose contemporary influences were the great writers of the 1920s, notably Boris Pilnyak, the Pilnyak of *The Naked Year*, Yevgeny Zamyatin, and Isaac Babel. But French remained his literary language. Serge's copious output as a translator was from Russian into French: works of Lenin, Trotsky, the founder of the Comintern Grigori Zinoviev, the pre-Bolshevik revolutionary Vera Figner (1852–1942), whose memoirs relate her twenty years of solitary confinement in a tsarist prison, and, among novelists and poets, Andrei Biely, Fyodor Gladkov, and Vladimir Mayakovsky. And his own books were all written in French. A Russian writer who writes in French—it means that Serge remains absent, even as a footnote, from the histories of both modern French and Russian literature.

Is it because whatever stature he had as a literary writer was always politicized, that is, viewed as a moral achievement? His was the literary voice of a righteous political militancy, a narrowing prism through which to view a body of work that has other, nondidactic claims on our attention.

During the late 1920s and the 1930s he had been a much-published writer, at least in France, with an ardent if small constituency—a political constituency, of course, mainly of the Trotskyist persuasion. But in the last years, after Serge had been excommunicated by Trotsky, that constituency had abandoned him to the predictable calumnies of the pro–Soviet Popular Front press. And the socialist positions Serge espoused after arriving in Mexico in 1941, a year after Trotsky was axed by the executioner sent by Stalin, seemed to his remaining supporters to be indistinguishable from those of the social democrats. More isolated than ever, boycotted by both the right and the left back in postwar Western Europe, the ex-Bolshevik, ex-Trotskyist, anti-Communist Serge continued to write—mostly for the drawer. He did publish a short book, *Hitler versus Stalin*, collaborate with a Spanish comrade in exile on a political magazine (*Mundo*), and contribute regularly to a few magazines abroad, but—despite the efforts of admirers as influential as Dwight Macdonald in New York and Orwell in London to find him a publisher—two of Serge's last three novels, the late stories and poems, and the memoirs remained unpublished in any language until after, mostly decades after, his death.

Is it because there were too many dualities in his life? He was a militant, a world-improver, to the end, which made him anathema to the right (even if, as he noted in his journal in February 1944, "Problems no longer have their former beautiful simplicity: it was convenient to live on antinomies like socialism or capitalism"). But he was a knowledgeable enough anti-Communist to worry that the American and British governments had not grasped that Stalin's goal after 1945 was to take over all of Europe (at the cost of a third world war), and this, in the era of widespread pro-Soviet or anti-anti-Communist bias among intellectuals in Western Europe, made Serge a renegade, a reactionary, a warmonger. "All the right enemies," the old motto proclaims: Serge had too many enemies. As an ex-, now anti-, Communist, he was never penitent enough. He deplores but he does not regret. He has not given up on the idea of radical social change because of the totalitarian outcome of the Russian Revolution. For Serge—to this extent he agrees with Trotsky—the revolution was betrayed. He is not saying it was a tragic illusion, a catastrophe for the Russian people, from the beginning. (But might Serge have said this had he lived another decade or more? Probably.) Finally, he was a lifelong practicing intellectual, which seemed to trump his achievement as a novelist, and he was a passionate political activist, which did not enhance his credentials as a novelist either.

Is it because he continued to the end to identify himself as a revolutionary, a vocation that is now so discredited in the prosperous world? Is it because, most implausibly, he insisted on being hopeful—still? "Behind us," he wrote in 1943, in *Memoirs of a Revolutionary*, "lies a victorious revolution gone astray, several abortive attempts at revolution, and massacres in so great a number as to inspire a certain dizziness." And yet Serge declared that "those were the only roads possible for us." And insisted, "I have more confidence in mankind and in the future than ever before." Surely this could not have been true.

Is it because, embattled and defeated as he was, his literary work refused to take on the expected cargo of melancholy? His indomitability is not as attractive to us as a more anguished reckoning. In his fiction, Serge writes about the worlds he has lived in, not about himself. It is a voice that forbids itself the requisite tones of despair or contrition or bewilderment—literary tones, as most people understand them—although Serge's own situation was increasingly grim. By 1947 he was desperately trying to get out of Mexico, where, by the terms of his visa, he was banned from all political activity, and, since an American visa was out of the question because of his Communist Party membership in the 1920s, to return to France. At the same time, incapable of being uninterested, unstimulated, wherever he was, he became fascinated by what he had observed on several trips around the country of the indigenous cultures and the landscape, and had begun a book about Mexico. The end was miserable. Shabbily dressed, ill nourished, increasingly plagued by angina—worsened by the high altitude of Mexico City—he had a heart attack while out late one evening, hailed a taxi, and died in the back seat. The driver deposited him at a police station; it was two days before his family learned what had happened to him and were able to claim the body.

In short, there was nothing, ever, triumphant about his life, as much that of the eternal poor student as the militant on the run—unless one excepts the triumph of being immensely gifted and industrious as a writer; the triumph of being principled and also astute and therefore incapable of keeping company with the faithful and the cravenly gullible and the merely hopeful; the triumph of being incorruptible as well as brave and therefore on a different, lonely path from the liars and toadies and careerists; the triumph of being, after the early 1920s, right.

Because he was right, he has been punished as a writer of fiction. The truth of history crowds out the truth of fiction—as if one were obliged to choose between them . . .

•

Is it because the life was so steeped in historical drama as to overshadow the work? Indeed, some of his fervent supporters have asserted that Serge's greatest literary work was his own tumultuous, danger-filled, ethically stalwart life. Something similar has been said of Oscar Wilde, who himself could not resist the masochistic quip, "I put all my genius into my life; I put only my talent into my works." Wilde was mistaken, and so is this misguided compliment to Serge. As is the case with most major writers, Serge's books are better, wiser, more important than the person who wrote them. To think otherwise is to condescend to Serge and to the very questions—How shall one live? How can I make sense of my own life? How can life be made better for those who are oppressed?—he honored by his lucidity, his rectitude, his valor, his defeats. While it is true that literature, particularly nineteenth-century Russian literature, is the home of these questions, it is cynical—or merely philistine—to consider as literary a life lived in their light. That would be to denigrate both morality and literature. History, too.

English-language readers of Serge today have to think themselves back to a time when most people accepted that the course of their lives would be determined by history rather than psychology, public rather than private crises. It was history, a particular historical moment, that drove Serge's parents out of tsarist Russia: the wave of repressiveness and state terror that followed the assassination of Alexander II by Narodnaya Volya (People's Will), the terrorist branch of the populist movement, in 1881. Serge's scientist father, Leon Kibalchich, at that time an officer in the Imperial Guard, belonged to a military group sympathetic to the *narodnik* (populist) demands, and barely escaped being shot when the group was discovered. In his first refuge, Geneva, he met and married a radical student from St. Petersburg of Polish gentry origin, and the two were to spend the rest of the decade, in the words of their second-generation political exile son, commuting "in quest of their daily bread and of good libraries . . . between London (the British Museum), Paris, Switzerland, and Belgium."

Revolution was at the heart of the socialist exile culture into which Serge was born: the quintessential hope, the quintessential intensity. "The conversations of grown-ups dealt with trials, executions, escapes, and Siberian highways, with great ideas incessantly argued over, and with the latest books about these ideas." Revolution was the modern tragic drama. "On the walls of our humble and makeshift lodgings, there were always the portraits of men who had been hanged." (One portrait, surely, was of Nikolai Kibalchich, a distant relative of his father, who was among the five conspirators convicted of assassinating Alexander II.)

Revolution entailed danger, the risk of death, the likelihood of prison. Revolution entailed hardship, privation, hunger. "I think that if anyone had asked me at the age of twelve, 'What is life?' (and I often asked it of myself), I would have replied, 'I do not know, but I can see that it means "*Thou shalt think, thou shalt struggle, thou shalt be hungry.*"'"

And it was. To read Serge's memoirs is to be brought back to an era that seems very remote today in its introspective energies and passionate intellectual quests and code of self-sacrifice and immense hope: an era in which the twelve-year-olds of cultivated parents might normally ask themselves "What is life?" Serge's cast of mind was not, for that time, precocious. It was the household culture of several generations of voraciously well-read idealists, many from the Slavic countries—the children of Russian literature, as it were. Staunch believers in science and human betterment, they were to provide the troops for many of the radical movements of the first third of the twentieth century; and were to be used, disillusioned, betrayed, and, if they happened to live in the Soviet Union, put to death. In his memoirs Serge reports his friend Pilnyak saying to him in 1933: "There isn't a single thinking adult in this country who hasn't thought that he might get shot."

Starting in the late 1920s, the chasm between reality and propaganda widened drastically. It was the climate of opinion that made the courageous Romanian-born writer Panaït Istrati (1884–1935) consider withdrawing his truthful report on a sixteen-month stay in the Soviet Union in 1927–28, *Vers une autre flamme* (Toward Another Flame), at the behest of his powerful French literary patron, Romain Rolland, which, when he did publish it, was rejected by all his former friends and supporters in the literary world; and that led André Malraux in his capacity as editor at Gallimard to turn down the adversarial biography of Stalin by the Russian-born Boris Souvarine (1895–1984, real name: Boris Lifchitz) as inimical to the cause of the Spanish Republic. (Istrati and Souvarine, who were close friends of Serge, formed with him a kind of triumvirate of foreign-born francophone writers who, from the late 1920s on, assumed the thankless role of denouncing from the left—therefore prematurely—what was happening in the Soviet Union.) To many living in the Depression-afflicted capitalist world, it seemed impossible *not* to sympathize with the struggle of this vast backward country to survive and to create, according to its stated aims, a new society based on economic and social justice. André Gide was being only a bit florid when he wrote in his journal in April 1932 that he would be willing to die for the Soviet Union:

> In the abominable distress of the present world, new Russia's plan now seems to me salvation. There is nothing that does not persuade me of this! The miserable arguments of its enemies, far from convincing me, make my blood boil. And if my life were necessary to ensure the success of the USSR, I should give it at once . . . as have done, as will do, so many others, and without distinguishing myself from them.

As for what was actually happening in the USSR in 1932—this is how Serge began "The Hospital in Leningrad," a short story he wrote in Mexico City in 1946 that anticipates the narratives of Solzhenitsyn:

> In 1932 I was living in Leningrad . . . Those were dark times, of shortages in the cities and famine in the villages, of terror, secret murder, and persecution of industrial managers and engineers, peasants, the religious, and those opposed to the regime. I belonged to the last category, which meant that at night, even in the depths of sleep, I never ceased to listen for the noises on the staircase, for the ascending footsteps heralding my arrest.

In October 1932 Serge wrote to the Central Committee of the Party appealing to be allowed to emigrate; permission was refused. In March 1933 Serge was arrested again and after a term in the Lubyanka was sent into internal exile to Orenburg, a bleak town on the frontier between Russia and Kazakhstan. Serge's plight was the subject of immediate protests in Paris. At the International Writers' Congress for the Defense of Culture, a stellar gathering held in Paris in June 1935, presided over by Gide and Malraux, which was the climax of Comintern-designed efforts to mobilize unaffiliated progressive-minded writers in defense of the Soviet Union—this just as Stalin's program of framing and executing all the surviving members of the Bolshevik Old Guard was getting under way—"the case of Victor Serge" was raised by a number of delegates. The following year Gide, who was about to leave, with entourage, for a triumphal tour of the Soviet Union on which great propaganda importance had been placed, went to see the Soviet ambassador in Paris requesting Serge's release. Rolland, on a return state visit to Russia, brought up the case with Stalin himself.

In April 1936 Serge (with his teenage son) was taken from Orenburg to Moscow, stripped of his Soviet citizenship, reunited with his mentally fragile wife and their infant daughter, and put on a train to Warsaw—the sole instance during the era of the Great Terror when a writer was liberated (that is, expelled from Soviet Russia) as the result of a foreign campaign of support. Undoubtedly, it helped enormously that the Belgian-born Russian was considered a foreigner.

After reaching Brussels in late April, Serge published an "Open Letter" to Gide in the French magazine *Esprit,* thanking him for a recent approach he had made to the Soviet authorities to try to recover Serge's confiscated manuscripts, and evoking some Soviet realities Gide might not hear about during his tour, such as the arrest and murder of many writers and the total suppression of intellectual freedom. (Serge had already sought contact with Gide in early 1934, sending him a letter from Orenburg about their shared conceptions of freedom in literature.) The two writers were able to meet secretly several times after Gide's return, in Paris in November 1936 and in Brussels in January 1937. Serge's journal accounts of these meetings provide a poignant contrast: Gide the consummate insider, the master on whom the mantle of the Great Writer had descended, and Serge, the knight of lost causes, itinerant, impoverished, always in jeopardy. (Of course, Gide was wary of Serge—of being influenced, of being misled.)

The French writer of the period whom Serge does resemble—in the starkness of his rectitude, his incessant studiousness, his principled renunciation of comfort, possessions, security—is his younger contemporary and fellow political militant, Simone Weil. It is more than likely that they met in Paris in 1936, shortly after Serge's liberation, or in 1937. Since June 1934, right after his arrest, Weil had been among those committed to keeping alive "the case of Victor Serge" and making direct protests to the Soviet authorities. They had a close friend in common, Souvarine; both wrote regularly for the syndicalist magazine, *La Révolution prolétarienne*. Weil was well known to Trotsky—the twenty-five-year-old Weil had had an evening of face-to-face debate with Trotsky on his brief visit to Paris in December 1934, when Weil arranged for him to use an apartment belonging to her parents for a clandestine political meeting—and figures in a letter to Serge in July 1936 in response to the suggestion that she collaborate on the new magazine Serge hoped to found. And during Weil's two months in late summer 1936 as a volunteer with an international militia fighting for the Spanish Republic, her principal political contact, whom she saw upon arriving in Barcelona, was the dissident Communist Julián Gorkin, another close friend of Serge's.

Trotskyist comrades had been the most active campaigners for Serge's freedom, and while in Brussels Serge gave his adherence to the Fourth International—as the league of Trotsky's supporters called themselves—although he knew the movement did not advance a viable alternative to the Leninist doctrines and practices that had led to Stalinist tyranny. (For Trotsky, the crime was that the *wrong* people were being shot.) His departure for Paris in 1937 was followed by the open rift with Trotsky, who from his new, Mexican exile denounced Serge as a closet anarchist; out of respect and affection for Trotsky, Serge refused to return the attack. Unfazed by the obloquy of being perceived as a turncoat, a traitor to the left, he published more against-the-stream tracts and dossiers on the destiny of the revolution from Lenin to Stalin, and another novel, *Midnight in the Century* (1939), set five years earlier, mostly in a remote town resembling Orenburg to which persecuted members of the Left Opposition have been deported. It is the very first depiction in a novel of the Gulag—properly, GULAG, the acronym for that vast internal carceral empire whose official name in Russian translates as Chief Administration of Camps. *Midnight in the Century* is dedicated to comrades from the most honorable of the radical parties in the Spanish Republic, the dissenting Communist— that is, anti-Stalinist—Partido Obrero de Unificación Marx-

ista (POUM); its leader Andrés Nin, executed by Soviet
agents in 1937, was a cherished friend of Serge's.

In June 1940, after the German occupation of Paris,
Serge fled to the south of France, eventually reaching the haven
set up by the heroic Varian Fry, who, in the name of an American private group calling itself the Emergency Rescue Committee, was to help some two thousand scholars, writers, artists,
musicians, and scientists find an exit from Hitler's Europe.
There, in the villa outside Marseilles that its inmates—they
included André Breton, Max Ernst, and André Masson—
dubbed *Espervisa*, Serge continued work on the new, more
ambitious novel about the reign of state murder in Soviet
Russia he had begun in Paris in early 1940. When a Mexican
visa finally came through for Serge (Breton and the others
were all admitted to the United States), he set out in March
1941 on the long precarious sea voyage. Delayed for questioning, then jailed by Vichy government officials when the cargo
ship stopped in Martinique, delayed again for want of transit
visas in the Dominican Republic, where during the enforced
sojourn he wrote a political tract designed for a Mexican public (*Hitler versus Stalin*), and delayed again in Havana, where,
jailed once more, he went on with his novel, Serge did not
arrive in Mexico until September. He finished *The Case of
Comrade Tulayev* the following year.

At the beginning of the twenty-first century, nothing of
the novel's once controversial aura remains. No sane person
now can dispute the toll of suffering that the Bolshevik system inflicted on the Russian people. Then, the consensus was
elsewhere, producing the scandal of Gide's unfavorable report on his trip, *Return from the USSR* (1937): Gide remained
even after his death in 1951 the great left-wing writer who

had betrayed Spain. The attitude was reproduced in Sartre's notorious refusal to broach the subject of the Gulag on the grounds that it would discourage the just militancy of the French working class. (*"Il ne faut pas faire désespérer Billancourt."*) For most writers who identified with the left in those decades, or who simply thought of themselves as against war (and were appalled at the prospect of a third world war), condemning the Soviet Union was at the very least problematic.

As if to confirm the anxiety on the left, those who had no problem denouncing the Soviet Union seemed to be precisely those who had no qualms about being racist or anti-Semitic or contemptuous of the poor; illiberals, who had never heard the siren call of idealism or been moved to any active sympathy with the excluded and the persecuted. The vice president of a major American insurance company, who was also America's greatest twentieth-century poet, might welcome Serge's testimony. Thus section XIV of Wallace Stevens's magisterial long poem "Esthétique du mal," written in 1945, opens with:

> Victor Serge said, "I followed his argument
> With the blank uneasiness which one might feel
> In the presence of a logical lunatic."
> He said it of Konstantinov. Revolution
> Is the affair of logical lunatics.
> The politics of emotion must appear
> To be an intellectual structure.

That it seems odd to find Serge evoked in a poem of Stevens's suggests how thoroughly Serge has been forgotten, for he was indeed a considerable presence in some of the most influential serious magazines of the 1940s. Stevens is likely to have been a reader of *Partisan Review*, if not of Dwight Macdonald's maverick radical magazine *Politics*, which published Serge (and Simone Weil, too); Macdonald and his wife, Nancy, had been a lifeline, financially and otherwise, to Serge during the desperate months in Marseilles and the obstacle-ridden voyage, and went on with their assiduous help once Serge and his family were in Mexico. Sponsored by Macdonald, Serge had begun writing for *Partisan Review* in 1938 and continued to send articles from this last, improbable residence. In 1942 he became Mexican correspondent of the New York anti-Communist biweekly *The New Leader* (Macdonald strongly disapproved), and later began contributing—on Orwell's recommendation—to *Polemic* and to Cyril Connolly's *Horizon* in London.

Minority magazines; minority views. Excerpted first in *Partisan Review*, Czeslaw Milosz's masterly portraits of the mutilation of the writer's honor, the writer's conscience, under Communism, *The Captive Mind* (1953), was discounted by much of the American literary public as a work of Cold War propaganda by the hitherto unknown émigré Polish writer. Similar suspicions persisted into the 1970s: when Robert Conquest's implacable, irrefutable chronicle of the state slaughters of the 1930s, *The Great Terror*, appeared in 1969, the book could be regarded in many quarters as controversial— its conclusions perhaps unhelpful, its implications downright reactionary.

Those decades of turning a blind eye to what went on in Communist regimes, specifically the conviction that to criticize the Soviet Union was to give aid and comfort to fascists and warmongers, seem almost incomprehensible now. In the early twenty-first century, we have moved on to other illusions—other lies that intelligent people with good intentions and humane politics tell themselves and their supporters in order not to give aid and comfort to their enemies.

There have always been people to argue that the truth is sometimes inexpedient, counterproductive—a luxury. (This is known as thinking practically, or politically.) And on the other side, the well-intentioned are understandably reluctant to jettison commitments, views, and institutions in which much idealism has been invested. Situations do arise in which truth and justice may seem incompatible. And there may be even more resistance to perceiving the truth than there is to acknowledging the claims of justice. It seems all too easy for people *not* to recognize the truth, especially when it may mean having to break with, or be rejected by, a community that supplies a valued part of their identity.

A different outcome is possible if one hears the truth from someone to whom one is disposed to listen. How was the Marquis de Custine, during his five-month tour of Russia a century earlier, able—prophetically—to understand how central to this society were the extravagances of despotism and submissiveness and indefatigable lying for the benefit of foreigners, which he described in his journal in the form of letters, *Russia in 1839*? Surely it mattered that Custine's lover was Polish, the young Count Ignacy Gurowski, who must have been eager to tell him of the horrors of tsarist oppression. Why was Gide, among all the left-wing visitors to the Soviet Union in the 1930s, the one to remain unseduced by the rhetoric of Communist equality and revolutionary idealism?

Perhaps because he had been primed to detect the dishonesty and the fear of his hosts by the intrusive briefings of the unimpeachable Victor Serge.

Serge, modestly, says it only takes some clarity and independence to tell the truth. In *Memoirs of a Revolutionary*, he writes:

> I give myself credit for having seen clearly in a number of important situations. In itself, this is not so difficult to achieve, and yet it is rather unusual. To my mind, it is less a question of an exalted or shrewd intelligence, than of good sense, goodwill and a certain sort of courage to enable one to rise above both the pressures of one's environment and the natural inclination to close one's eyes to facts, a temptation that arises from our immediate interests and from the fear which problems inspire in us. A French essayist has said: "What is terrible when you seek the truth, is that you find it." You find it, and then you are no longer free to follow the biases of your personal circle, or to accept fashionable clichés.

"What is terrible when you seek the truth . . ." A dictum to be pinned above every writer's desk.

The ignominious obtuseness and lies of Dreiser, Rolland, Henri Barbusse, Louis Aragon, Beatrice and Sidney Webb, Halldór Laxness, Egon Erwin Kisch, Walter Duranty, Leon Feuchtwanger, and the like are mostly forgotten. And so are those who opposed them, who fought for the truth. The truth, once acquired, is ungrateful. We can't remember everyone. What is remembered is not testimony but . . . literature. The presumptive case for exempting Serge from the oblivion that awaits most heroes of truth lies, finally, in the excellence of his fiction, above all *The Case of Comrade Tulayev*. But to be a literary writer perceived only or mainly as a didactic writer; to be a writer without a country, a country in whose literary canon his fiction would find a place—these elements of Serge's complex fate continue to obscure this admirable, enthralling book.

·

Fiction, for Serge, is truth—the truth of self-transcendence, the obligation to give voice to those who are mute or have been silenced. He disdained novels of private life, most of all autobiographical novels. "Individual existences were of no interest to me—particularly my own," he remarks in the *Memoirs*. In a journal entry (March 1944), Serge explains the larger reach of his idea of fictional truth:

> Perhaps the deepest source is the feeling that marvelous life is passing, flying, slipping inexorably away and the desire to detain it in flight. It was this desperate feeling that drove me, around the age of sixteen, to note the precious instant, that made me discover that *existence* (human, "divine") *is memory*. Later, with the enrichment of the personality, one discovers its limits, the poverty and the shackles of the self, one discovers that one has only one life, an individuality forever circumscribed, but which contains many possible destinies, and . . . mingles . . . with the other human existences, and the earth, the creatures, everything. Writing then becomes a quest of poly-personality, a way of living diverse destinies, of penetrating into others, of communi-

cating with them . . . of escaping from the ordinary limits of the self . . . (Doubtless there are other kinds of writers, individualists, who only seek their own self-assertion and can't see the world except through themselves.)

The point of fiction was storytelling, world-evoking. This credo drew Serge as a fiction writer to two seemingly incompatible ideas of the novel.

One is the historical panorama, in which single novels have their place as episodes of a comprehensive story. The story, for Serge, was heroism and injustice in the first half of the European twentieth century and could have started with a novel set in anarchist circles in France just before 1914 (about which he did finish a memoir, seized by the GPU). Of the novels Serge was able to complete, the time line runs from the First through the Second World War—that is, from *Men in Prison*, written in Leningrad at the end of the 1920s and published in Paris in 1930, to *Les années sans pardon* (The Pitiless Years), his last novel, written in Mexico in 1946 and not published until 1971, in Paris. (It has yet to be translated into English.) *The Case of Comrade Tulayev*, whose material is the Great Terror of the 1930s, comes toward the end of the cycle. Characters recur—a classic feature of novels, like some of Balzac's, conceived as a sequence—though not as many as one might expect, and none of them an alter ego, a stand-in for Serge himself. The High Commissar for Security Erchov, the prosecutor Fleischman, the loathsome apparatchik Zvyeryeva, and the virtuous Left Oppositionist Ryzhik of *The Case of Comrade Tulayev* had all figured in *Conquered City* (1932), Serge's third novel, which takes place during the siege of Petrograd, and, probably, in the lost novel, *La tourmente* (The Storm), which was the sequel to *Conquered City*. (Ryzhik is also an important character, and Fleischman a minor one, in *Midnight in the Century*.)

Of this project we have only fragments. But if Serge did not commit himself doggedly to a chronicle, like Solzhenitsyn's sequence of novels about the Lenin era, it is not simply because Serge lacked the time to complete his sequence, but because another idea of the novel was at work, somewhat subverting the first. Solzhenitsyn's historical novels are all of a piece from a literary point of view, and none the better for that. Serge's novels illustrate several different conceptions of how to narrate and to what end. The "I" of *Men in Prison* (1930) is a medium for giving voice to the others, many others; it is a novel of compassion, of solidarity. "I don't want to write memoirs," he said in a letter to Istrati, who did the preface to Serge's first novel. The second novel, *The Birth of Our Power* (1931), uses a mix of voices—the first-person "I" and "we" and an omniscient third person. The multivolume chronicle, the novel as sequel, was not the best vessel for Serge's development as a literary writer but remained a kind of default position from which, always working under harassment and financial strain, he could generate new fictional tasks.

Serge's literary affinities, and many of his friendships, were with the great modernists of the 1920s, such as Pilnyak, Zamyatin, Sergei Esenin, Mayakovsky, Pasternak, Daniil Kharms (his brother-in-law), and Osip Mandelstam—rather than with realists like Gorky, a relative on his mother's side, and Alexei Tolstoy. But in 1928, when Serge started writing fiction, the miraculous new literary era was virtually over, killed by the censors, and soon the writers themselves, most of them, were to be arrested and killed or to commit suicide. The broad-canvas novel, the narrative with multiple voices (another example: *Noli Me Tangere* by the late-nineteenth-century Filipino revolutionary José Rizal), might well be the preferred form of a writer with a powerful political consciousness—the political consciousness that was certainly not wanted in the Soviet Union, where, Serge knew, there was no chance of his being translated and published. But it is also the form of some of the enduring works of literary modernism and has spawned several new fictional genres. Serge's third novel, *Conquered City*, is a brilliant work in one of these genres, the novel with a city as protagonist (as *Men in Prison* had as protagonist "that terrible machine, prison")—clearly influenced by Biely's *Petersburg*, and by *Manhattan Transfer* (he cites Dos Passos as an influence), and possibly by *Ulysses*, a book he greatly admired.

"I had the strong conviction of charting a new road for the novel," Serge says in the *Memoirs*. One way in which Serge is not charting a new road is his view of women, reminiscent of the great Soviet films about revolutionary ideals, from Eisenstein to Alexei Gherman. In this entirely men-centered society of challenge—and ordeal, and sacrifice—women barely exist, at least not positively, except through being the love objects or wards of very busy men. For revolution, as Serge describes it, is itself a heroic, masculinist enterprise, invested with the values of virility: courage, daring, endurance, decisiveness, independence, ability to be brutal. An attractive woman, someone warm, cherishing, sturdy, often a victim, cannot have these manly characteristics; therefore she cannot be other than a revolutionary's junior partner. The one powerful woman in *The Case of Comrade Tulayev*, the Bolshevik prosecutor Zvyeryeva (who will soon have her turn to be arrested and killed), is repeatedly characterized by her pathetically needy sexuality (in one scene she is shown masturbating) and physical repulsiveness. All the men in the novel, villainous or not, have forthright carnal needs and unaffected sexual self-confidence.

The Case of Comrade Tulayev relates a set of stories, of fates, in a densely populated world. Besides the cast of supportive women, there are at least eight major characters: two emblems of disaffection, Kostia and Romachkin, lowly bachelor clerks who share a single room with a partition in a communal apartment in Moscow—they open the novel—and the veteran loyalists, careerists, and sincere Communists, Ivan Kondratiev, Artyem Makeyev, Stefan Stern, Maxim Erchov, Kiril Rublev, old Ryzhik, who are, one by one, arrested, interrogated, and sentenced to die. (Only Kondratiev is spared, and sent to a remote post in Siberia, by an arbitrarily benign whim of "The Chief," as Stalin is called in the novel.) Whole lives are portrayed, each of which could make a novel. The account of Makeyev's ingeniously staged arrest while attending the opera (at the end of Chapter 4) is in itself a short story worthy of Chekhov. And the drama of Makeyev—his antecedents, ascent to power (he is governor of Kurgansk), sudden arrest on a visit to Moscow, imprisonment, interrogation, confession—is only one of the plots elaborated in *The Case of Comrade Tulayev*.

No interrogator is a major character. Among the minor characters is Serge's fictional epitome of the fellow traveler of influence. In a late scene, set in Paris, "Professor Passereau, famous in two hemispheres, President of the Congress for the

Defense of Culture," tells the young émigré, Xenia Popov, vainly seeking his intervention on behalf of the most sympathetic of Serge's Old Bolshevik protagonists: "For the justice of your country I have a respect which is absolute . . . If Rublev is innocent, the Supreme Tribunal will accord him justice." As for the eponymous Tulayev, the high government official whose murder sets off the arrest and execution of the others, he makes only the briefest appearance early in the novel. He is there to be shot.

Serge's Tulayev, at any rate his murder and its consequences, seems obviously to point back to Sergei Kirov, the head of the Leningrad Party organization, whose assassination in his office on December 1, 1934, by a young Party member named Leon Nikolayev became Stalin's pretext for the years of slaughter that followed, which decimated the loyal Party membership and killed or kept imprisoned for decades millions of ordinary citizens. It may be difficult not to read *The Case of Comrade Tulayev* as a roman à clef, though Serge in a prefatory note explicitly warns against doing just that. "This novel," he writes, "belongs to the domain of literary fiction. The truth created by the novelist cannot be confounded, in any degree whatever, with the truth of the historian or chronicler." One can hardly imagine Solzhenitsyn prefacing one of his Lenin-novels with such a disclaimer. But perhaps one should take Serge at his word—noting that he set his novel in 1939. The arrests and trials in *The Case of Comrade Tulayev* are fictional successors to, rather than a fictional synthesis of, the actual Moscow trials of 1936, 1937, and 1938.

Serge is not just pointing out that the truth of the novelist differs from the truth of the historian. He is asserting, here only implicitly, the superiority of the novelist's truth. Serge had made the bolder claim in the letter to Istrati about *Men in Prison*: a novel that, despite "the convenient use of the first person singular," is "not about me," and in which "I don't even want to stick too close to things I have actually seen." The novelist, Serge continues, is after "a richer and more general truth than the truth of observation." That truth "sometimes coincides almost photographically with certain things I have seen; sometimes it differs from them in every respect."

To assert the superiority of the truth of fiction is a venerable literary commonplace (its earliest formulation is in Aristotle's *Poetics*) and in the mouths of many writers sounds glib and even self-serving: a permission claimed by the novelist to be inaccurate, or partial, or arbitrary. To say that the assertion voiced by Serge has nothing of this quality is to point to the evidence of his novels, their incontestable sincerity and intelligence applied to *lived* truths re-created in the form of fiction.

The Case of Comrade Tulayev has never enjoyed a fraction of the fame of Koestler's *Darkness at Noon* (1940), a novel with ostensibly the same subject, which makes the opposite claim, for the correspondence of fiction to historical reality. "The life of the man N. S. Rubashov is a synthesis of the lives of a number of men who were victims of the so-called Moscow Trials," the prefatory note to *Darkness at Noon* advises the reader. (Rubashov is thought to be mostly based on Nikolai Bukharin, with something of Karl Radek.) But synthesis is exactly the limitation of Koestler's chamber drama, which is both political argument and psychological portrait. An entire era is seen through the prism of one person's ordeal of confinement and interrogation, interspersed with passages of recollection; flashbacks. The novel opens with Rubashov, ex–Commissar of the People, being pushed into his cell and the door slamming behind him, and ends with the executioner arriving with the handcuffs, the descent to the prison cellar, and the bullet in the back of the head. (It is not surprising that *Darkness at Noon* could be made into a Broadway play.) The revelation of *how*—that is, by what arguments rather than by physical torture—Zinoviev, Kamenev, Radek, Bukharin, and the other ruling members of the Bolshevik elite could be induced to confess to the absurd charges of treason brought against them is the story of *Darkness at Noon*.

Serge's polyphonic novel, with its many trajectories, has a much more complicated view of character, of the interweaving of politics and private life, and of the terrible procedures of Stalin's inquisition. And it casts a much wider intellectual net. (An example: Rublev's analysis of the revolutionary generation.) Of those arrested, all but one will eventually confess— Ryzhik, who remains defiant, prefers to go on a hunger strike and die—but only one resembles Koestler's Rubashov: Erchov, who is persuaded to render one last service to the Party by admitting that he was part of the conspiracy to assassinate Tulayev. "Every Man Has His Own Way of Drowning" is the title of one of the chapters.

The Case of Comrade Tulayev is a far less conventional novel than are *Darkness at Noon* and *1984*, whose portraits of totalitarianism have proved so unforgettable—perhaps because those novels have a single protagonist and tell a single story. One need not think of either Koestler's Rubashov or Orwell's Winston Smith as a hero; the fact that both novels stay with their protagonists from beginning to end forces the reader's identification with the archetypal victim of totalitarian tyranny. If Serge's novel can be said to have a hero, it is someone, present only in the first and last chapters, who is not a victim: Kostia, the actual assassin of Tulayev, who remains unsuspected.

Murder, killing, is in the air. It is what history is about. A Colt revolver is bought from a shady purveyor—for no particular reason, except that it is a magical object, bluish-black steel, and feels potent concealed in the pocket. One day its purchaser, the insignificant Romachkin, a miserable soul and also (in his own eyes) "a pure man whose one thought was justice," is walking near the Kremlin wall at the moment when a uniformed figure, "his uniform bare of insignia, his face hard, bristlingly mustached, and inconceivably sensual," emerges, followed by two men in civilian clothes, a mere thirty feet away, then stops six feet away to light a pipe, and Romachkin realizes he has been presented with an opportunity to shoot Stalin ("the Chief") himself. He doesn't. Disgusted by his own cowardice, he gives the gun away to Kostia, who, out on a snowy night, observes a stout man in a fur-lined coat and astrakhan cap with a briefcase under his arm getting out of a powerful black car that has just pulled up in front of a private residence, hears him addressed by the chauffeur as Comrade Tulayev— Tulayev of the Central Committee, Kostia realizes, he of "the mass deportations" and "the university purges"—sees him sending the car away (in fact, Tulayev does not intend to enter his house but to continue on foot to a sexual assignation), at which moment, as if in a trance, a fit of absence, the gun comes out of Kostia's pocket. The gun explodes, a sudden clap of thunder in a dead silence. Tulayev falls to the sidewalk. Kostia flees through the narrow quiet streets.

Serge makes the murder of Tulayev nearly involuntary, like the murder of an unknown man at the beach for which the protagonist of Camus's *The Stranger* (1942) stands trial. (It seems very unlikely that Serge, marooned in Mexico, could have read Camus's novel, published clandestinely in Occupied France, before finishing his own.) The affectless antihero of Camus's novel is a kind of victim, first of all in his unawareness of his actions. In contrast, Kostia is full of feeling, and his *acte gratuit* is both sincere and irrational: his awareness of the iniquity of the Soviet system acts *through* him. However, the unlimited violence of the system makes his act of violence impossible to avow. When, toward the end of the novel, Kostia, tormented by how much further injustice has been unleashed by his deed, sends a written confession, unsigned, to the chief prosecutor on the Tulayev case, he, Fleischman—only a few steps from being arrested himself—burns the letter, collects the ashes and crushes them under his thumb, and "with as much relief as gloomy sarcasm" says half aloud to himself: "The Tulayev case is closed." Truth, including a true confession, has no place in the kind of tyranny that the revolution has become.

To assassinate a tyrant is an accomplishment that may evoke Serge's anarchist past, and Trotsky was not entirely wrong when he accused Serge of being more anarchist than Marxist. But he had never supported anarchist violence: it was his libertarian convictions that had made Serge, early on, an anarchist. His life as a militant gave him a profound experience of death. That experience is most keenly expressed in *Conquered City*, with its scenes of killing as compulsion, orgy, political necessity, but death presides over all Serge's novels.

"It is not for us to be admirable," declares the voice of a woeful encomium to revolutionary hard-heartedness, "Meditation during an Air-Raid," in *Birth of Our Power.* We revolutionaries "must be precise, clear-sighted, strong, unyielding, armed: like machines." (Of course, Serge is totally committed, by temperament and by principle, to what is admirable.) Serge's master theme is revolution and death: to make a revolution one must be pitiless, one must accept the inevitability of killing the innocent as well as the guilty. There is no limit to the sacrifices that the revolution can demand. Sacrifice of others; sacrifice of oneself. For that hubris, the sacrificing of so many others in revolution's cause, virtually guarantees that eventually the same pitiless violence will be turned on those who made the revolution. In Serge's fiction, the revolutionary is, in the strictest, classical sense, a tragic figure—a hero who will do, who is obliged to do, *what is wrong*; and in so doing courts, and will endure, retribution, punishment.

But in Serge's best fiction—these are much more than "political novels"—the tragedy of revolution is set in a larger frame. Serge is devoted to showing the illogic of history and of human motivation and the course of individual lives, which can never be said to be either deserved or undeserved. Thus *The Case of Comrade Tulayev* ends with the contrasting destinies of its two lesser lives: Romachkin, the man obsessed by justice, who lacked the courage, or the absence of mind, to kill Stalin and has become a valued bureaucrat (so far not purged) in Stalin's terror state, and Kostia, Tulayev's assassin, the man who protested in spite of himself and has escaped into humble agricultural work in Russia's far east, and mindlessness, and new love.

The truth of the novelist—unlike the truth of the historian—allows for the arbitrary, the mysterious, the under-motivated. The truth of fiction replenishes: for there is much more than politics, and more than the vagaries of human feeling. The truth of fiction embodies, as in the pungent physicalness of Serge's descriptions of people and of landscapes. The truth of fiction depicts that for which one can never be consoled and displaces it with a healing openness to everything finite and cosmic.

"I want to blow out the moon," says the little girl at the end of Pilnyak's "The Tale of the Unextinguished Moon" (1926), which re-creates as fiction one of the first liquidations of a possible future rival ordered by Stalin (here called "Number One"): the murder, in 1925, of Trotsky's successor as the head of the Red Army, Mikhail Frunze, who was forced to undergo unnecessary surgery, and died, as planned, on the operating table. (Pilnyak's subsequent cave-in to Stalinist literary directives in the 1930s did not keep him from being shot in 1938.) In a world of unbearable cruelty and injustice, it seems as if all of nature should rhyme with grief and loss. And indeed, Pilnyak relates, the moon, as if in response to the challenge, vanishes. "The moon, plump as a merchant's wife, swam behind clouds, wearying of the chase." But the moon is not to be extinguished. Neither is the saving indifference, the saving larger view, that is the novelist's or the poet's— which does not obviate the truth of political understanding, but tells us there is more than politics, more, even, than history. Bravery . . . and indifference . . . and sensuality . . . and the living creatural world . . . and pity, pity for all, remain unextinguished.

Outlandish

On Halldór Laxness's
Under the Glacier

The long prose fiction called the novel, for want of a better name, has yet to shake off the mandate of its own normality as promulgated in the nineteenth century: to tell a story peopled by characters whose options and destinies are those of ordinary, so-called real life. Narratives that deviate from this artificial norm and tell other kinds of stories, or appear not to tell much of a story at all, draw on traditions that are more venerable than those of the nineteenth century, but still, to this day, seem innovative or ultraliterary or bizarre. I am thinking of novels that proceed largely through dialogue; novels that are relentlessly jocular (and therefore seem exaggerated) or didactic; novels whose characters spend most of their time musing to themselves or debating with a captive interlocutor about spiritual and intellectual issues; novels that tell of the initiation of an ingenuous young person into mystifying wisdom or revelatory abjection; novels with characters who have supernatural options, like shape-shifting and resurrection; novels that evoke imaginary geography. It seems odd to describe *Gulliver's Travels* or *Candide* or *Tristram Shandy* or *Jacques the Fatalist and His Master* or *Alice in Wonderland* or Gershenzon and Ivanov's *Correspondence from Two Corners* or Kafka's *The Castle or* Hesse's *Steppenwolf* or Woolf's *The Waves* or Olaf Stapledon's *Odd John* or Gombrowicz's *Ferdydurke* or Calvino's *Invisible Cities* or, for that matter, porno narratives simply as novels. To make the point that these occupy the outlying precincts of the novel's main tradition, special labels are invoked.

Science fiction.
Tale, fable, allegory.
Philosophical novel.
Dream novel.
Visionary novel.
Literature of fantasy.
Wisdom lit.
Spoof.
Sexual turn-on.

Convention dictates that we slot many of the last centuries' perdurable literary achievements into one or another of these categories.

The only novel I know that fits into all of them is Halldór Laxness's wildly original, morose, uproarious *Under the Glacier*.

·

Science fiction first.

In 1864 Jules Verne published *Journey to the Center of the Earth*, the charming narrative of the adventures of a

party of three, led by a German professor of mineralogy—
the irascible mad-scientist type—who have lowered themselves into an extinct volcanic crater on a glacier in Iceland,
Snæfells, and eventually exit upward through the mouth of
an active volcano on another island, Stromboli, off the coast
of Sicily. Just over a hundred years later, in 1968, Snæfells is
again the designated portal of another unlikely fictional mission in a novel by Iceland's own Halldór Laxness, written with
full mocking awareness of how the French father of science
fiction had colonized the Icelandic site. This time, instead of
a journey into the earth, mere proximity to the glacier opens
up access to unexpected cosmic mysteries.

Imagining the exceptional, often understood as the miraculous, the magical, or the supernatural, is a perennial job
of storytelling. One tradition proposes a physical place of
entry—a cave or a tunnel or a hole—which leads to a freak-
ish or enchanted kingdom with an alternative normality. In
Laxness's story, a sojourn near Snæfells does not call for the
derring-do of a descent, a penetration, since, as Icelanders
who inhabit the region know, the glacier itself is the center of
the universe. The supernatural—the center—is present on the
surface, in the costume of everyday life in a village whose er-
rant pastor has ceased to conduct services or baptize children
or bury the dead. Christianity—Iceland's confession is Evangelical Lutheran—is the name of what is normal, historical,
local.* (The agricultural Viking island converted to Christianity on a single day at the Althing, the world's oldest national parliament, in 999.) But what is happening in remote
Snæfells is abnormal, cosmic, global.

*Translated literally, the original Icelandic title reads *Christianity at Glacier.*

Science fiction proposes two essential challenges to conventional ideas of time and place. One is that time may be abridged, or become "unreal." The other is that there are special places in the universe where familiar laws that govern identity and morality are violated. In more strenuous forms of science fiction, these are places where good and evil contend. In benign versions of this geographical exceptionalism, these are places where wisdom accumulates. Snæfells is such a place—or so it is stipulated. People lead their mundane, peculiar lives, seemingly unfazed by the knowledge of the uniqueness of where they live: "No one in these parts doubts that the glacier is the center of the universe." Snæfells has become a laboratory of the new, the unsettling: a place of secret pilgrimage.

.

As a species of storytelling, science fiction is a modern variant of the literature of allegorical quest. It often takes the form of a perilous or mysterious journey, recounted by a venturesome but ignorant traveler who braves the obstacles to confront another reality that is charged with revelations. He, for it is always a he, stands for humanity as apprenticeship, since women are not thought to be representative of human beings in general but only of women. A woman can represent Women. Only a man can stand for Man or Mankind—everybody. Of course, a female protagonist can represent The Child—as in *Alice in Wonderland*—but not The Adult.

Thus, both *Journey to the Center of the Earth* and *Under the Glacier* have as protagonist and narrator a good-natured, naïve young man who submits his will to that of an older authority figure. Verne's narrator is the eminent Professor

Lidenbrock's orphaned nephew and assistant, Axel, who cannot refuse the invitation to accompany his uncle and an Icelandic guide on this adventure, though he is sure that it will cost them their lives. In Laxness's novel, which opens on a note of parody, the narrator is a nameless youth whom the Bishop of Iceland in Reykjavík wants to send to the village at the foot of Snæfells Glacier "to conduct the most important investigation at that world-famous mountain since the days of Jules Verne." He is to find out what has happened to the parish there, whose minister—Pastor Jón Jónsson, known as Prímus— has not drawn his salary for twenty years. Is Christianity still being practiced? There are rumors that the church is boarded up and no services held, that the pastor lives with someone who is not his wife, that the pastor has allowed a corpse to be lodged in the glacier.

The Bishop tells the young man he has sent countless letters to Prímus. No answer. He wants the young man to make a brief trip to the village, talk to the pastor, and take the true measure of his spiritual dereliction.

·

And beyond science fiction.

Under the Glacier is at least as much a philosophical novel and a dream novel. It is also one of the funniest books ever written. But these genres—science fiction, philosophical novel, dream novel, comic novel—are not as distinct as one might suppose.

For instance, both science fictions and philosophical novels need principal characters who are skeptical, recalcitrant, astonished, ready to marvel. The science fiction novel usually begins with the proposal of a journey. The philosoph-

ical novel may dispense with the journey—thinking is a seden-
tary occupation—but not with the classical male pair: the
master who asks and the servant who is certain, the one who
is puzzled and the one who thinks he has the answers.

In the science fiction novel, the protagonist must first
contend with his terrors. Axel's dread at being enrolled by his
uncle in this daft venture of descending into the bowels of
the earth is more than understandable. The question is not
what he will learn but whether he will survive the physical
shocks to which he will be subjected. In the philosophical
novel, the element of fear—and true danger—is minimal, if
it exists at all. The question is not survival but what one can
know, and if one can know anything at all. Indeed, the very
conditions of knowing become the subject of rumination.

In *Under the Glacier*, when the generic Naïve Young
Man receives his charge from the Bishop of Iceland to inves-
tigate the goings-on at Snæfells, he protests that he is completely unqualified for the mission. In particular—"for the sake
of appearances," he adds slyly—he instances his youth and
lack of authority to scrutinize a venerable old man's discharge
of his pastoral duties, when the words of the Bishop himself
have been ignored. Is the young man—the reader is told that
he is twenty-five and a student—at least a theological student? Not even. Has he plans to be ordained? Not really. Is he
married? No. (In fact, as we learn, he's a virgin.) A problem
then? No problem. To the worldly Bishop, the lack of qualifi-
cations of this Candide-like young Icelander is what makes
him the right person. If the young man were qualified, he
might be tempted to judge what he sees.

All the young man has to do, the Bishop explains, is

keep his eyes open, listen, and take notes; that the Bishop knows he can do, having observed the young man taking notes in shorthand at a recent synod meeting, and also using the—what's it called? a phonograph? It was a tape recorder, says the young man. And then, the Bishop continues, write it all up. What you saw and heard. Don't judge.

Laxness's novel is both the narrative of the journey and the report.

·

A philosophical novel generally proceeds by setting up a quarrel with the very notion of novelistic invention. One common device is to present the fiction as a document, something found or recovered, often after its author's death or disappearance: research or writings in manuscript; a diary; a cache of letters.

In *Under the Glacier*, the antifictional fiction is that what the reader has in hand is a document prepared or in preparation, submitted rather than found. Laxness's ingenious design deploys two notions of "a report": the report to the reader, sometimes in the first person, sometimes in the form of unadorned dialogue, which is cast as the material, culled from taped conversations and observations from shorthand notebooks, of a report that is yet to be written up and presented to the Bishop. The status of Laxness's narrative is something like a Moebius strip: report to the reader and report to the Bishop continue to inflect each other. The first-person voice is actually a hybrid voice; the young man—whose name is never divulged—frequently refers to himself in the third person. "The undersigned," he calls himself at first. Then "Emissary

of the Bishop," abbreviated to "EmBi," which quickly becomes "Embi." And he remains the undersigned or Embi
throughout the novel.

The arrival of the emissary of the Bishop of Iceland is
expected, Embi learns when he reaches the remote village
by bus one spring day; it's early May. From the beginning,
Embi's picturesque informants, secretive and garrulous in the
usual rural ways, accept his right to interrogate them without
either curiosity or antagonism. Indeed, one running gag in
the novel is that the villagers tend to address him as "Bishop."
When he protests that he is a mere emissary, they reply that
his role makes him spiritually consubstantial with the Bishop.
Bishop's emissary, Bishop—same thing.

And so this earnest, self-effacing young man—who
refers to himself in the third person, out of modesty, not for
the usual reason—moves from conversation to conversation,
for this is a novel of talk, debate, sparring, rumination. Everyone whom he interviews has pagan or post-Christian ideas about
time and obligation and the energies of the universe: the little village at the foot of the glacier is in full spiritual molt.
Present, in addition to elusive Pastor Jón—who, when Embi
finally catches up with him (he now earns a living as the jack-
of-all-trades for the whole district), shocks the youth with his
sly theological observations—is an international conclave of
gurus, the most eminent of which is Dr. Godman Sýngmann
from Ojai, California. Embi does not aspire to be initiated
into any of these heresies. He wishes to remain a guest, an observer, an amanuensis: his task is to be a mirror. But when eros
enters in the form of the pastor's mysterious wife, Úa, he becomes—first reluctantly, then surrendering eagerly—a par-

ticipant. He wants something. Longing erupts. The journey becomes *his* journey, *his* initiation, after all. ("The report has not just become part of my own blood—the quick of my life has fused into one with the report.") The journey ends when the revelatory presence proves to be a phantom and vanishes. The utopia of erotic transformation was only a dream, after all. But it is hard to undo an initiation. The protagonist will have to labor to return to reality.

．

Dream novel.

Readers will recognize the distinctive dream world of Scandinavian folk mythology, in which the spiritual quest of a male is empowered and sustained by the generosity and elusiveness of the eternal feminine. A sister to Solveig in Ibsen's *Peer Gynt* and to Indra in Strindberg's *A Dream Play*, Úa is the irresistible woman who transforms: the witch, the whore, the mother, the sexual initiator, wisdom's fount. Úa gives her age as fifty-two, which makes her twice as old as Embi—the same difference of age, she points out, as Santa Teresa and San Juan de la Cruz when *they* first met—but in fact she is a shape-shifter, immortal. Eternity in the form of a woman. Úa has been Pastor Jón's wife (although she is a Roman Catholic), the madam of a brothel in Buenos Aires, and a nun, and had countless other identities. She appears to speak all the principal languages. She knits incessantly: mittens, she explains, for the fishermen of Peru. Perhaps most peculiarly, she has been dead, conjured into a fish and preserved up on the glacier until a few days earlier and has now been resurrected by Pastor Jón and is about to become Embi's lover.

This is perennial mythology, Nordic style, not just a spoof of the myth. As Strindberg put it in the preface to his forgotten masterpiece, *A Dream Play*: "Time and space do not exist." Time and space are mutable in the dream novel, the dream play. Time can always be revoked. Space is multiple.

Strindberg's timelessness and placelessness are not ironic, as they are for Laxness, who scatters a few impure details in *Under the Glacier*—historical grit that reminds the reader this is not only the folktime of Nordic mythology but also that landmark year of self-loving apocalyptic yearning: 1968. The book's author, who published his first novel when he was seventeen and wrote some sixty novels in the course of his long and far from provincial life (he died at ninety-five), was already sixty-six years old. Born in rural Iceland, he lived in the United States in the late 1920s, mostly in Hollywood. He spent time in the Soviet Union in the 1930s. He had already accepted a Stalin Peace Prize (1952) and a Nobel Prize in Literature (1955). He was known for epic novels about poor Icelandic farmers. He was a writer with a conscience. He had been obtusely philo-Soviet (for decades) and was then interested in Taoism. He read Sartre's *Saint Genet* and publicly decried the American bases in Iceland and the American war on Vietnam. But *Under the Glacier* does not reflect any of these literal concerns. It is a work of supreme derision and freedom and wit. It is like nothing else Laxness ever wrote.

·

Comic novel.

The comic novel also relies on the naïve narrator: the person of incomplete understanding, and inappropriate, indefatigable cheerfulness or optimism. Pastor Jón, Úa, the villagers: everyone tells Embi he doesn't understand. "Aren't you just a tiny bit limited, my little one?" Úa observes tenderly. To be often wrong, but never disheartened; gamely acknowledging one's mistakes, and soldiering on—this is an essentially comic situation. (The comedy of candor works best when the protagonist is young, as in Stendhal's autobiographical *La Vie de Henry Brulard*.) An earnest, innocent hero to whom preposterous things happen attempts, for the most part successfully, to take them in his stride. That the nameless narrator sometimes says "I" and sometimes speaks of himself in the third person introduces a weird note of depersonalization, which also evokes laughter. The rollicking mixture of voices cuts through the pathos; it expresses the fragile false confidence of the comic hero.

What is comic is not being surprised at what is astonishing or absurd. The Bishop's mandate—to underreact to whatever his young emissary is to encounter—sets up an essentially comic scenario. Embi always underreacts to the preposterous situations in which he finds himself: for example, the food that he is offered every day by the pastor's housekeeper during his stay—nothing but cakes.

Think of the films of Buster Keaton and Harry Langdon; think of the writings of Gertrude Stein. The basic elements of a comic situation: deadpan; repetition; defect of affectivity; deficit (apparent deficit, anyway) of understanding, of what one is doing (making the audience superior to the state of mind being represented); naïvely solemn behavior; inappropriate cheerfulness—all of which give the impression of childlikeness.

The comic is also cruel. This is a novel about humiliation—the humiliation of the hero. He endures frustration, sleep deprivation, food deprivation. (No, the church is not open now. No, you can't eat now. No, I don't know where the pastor is.) It is an encounter with a mysterious authority that will not reveal itself. Pastor Jón appears to have abdicated his authority by ceasing to perform the duties of a minister and choosing instead to be a mechanic, but he has actually sought access to a much larger authority—mystical, cosmic, galactic. Embi has stumbled into a community that is a coven of authority figures, whose provenance and powers he never manages to decipher. Of course they are rogues, charlatans—and they are not; or at any rate, their victims, the credulous, deserve them (as in a much darker Hungarian novel about spiritual charlatans and rural dupes, Krasznahorkai's *Sátántangó*). Wherever Embi turns, he does not understand, and he is not being helped to understand. The pastor is away, the church is closed. But unlike, say, K in Kafka's *The Castle*, Embi does not suffer. For all his humiliations, he does not appear to feel anguish. The novel has a weird coldness. It is both cruel and merry.

·

Visionary novel.

The comic novel and the visionary novel also have something in common: nonexplicitness. An aspect of the comic is meaninglessness and inanity, which is a great resource of comedy, and also of spirituality—at least in the Oriental (Taoist) version that attracted Laxness.

At the beginning of the novel, the young man continues for a bit to protest his inability to carry out the Bishop's mission. What am I to say? he asks. What am I to do?

The Bishop replies: "One should simply say and do as little as possible. Keep your eyes peeled. Talk about the weather. Ask what sort of summer they had last year, and the year before that. Say that the Bishop has rheumatism. If any others have rheumatism, ask where it affects them. Don't try to put anything right."

More of the Bishop's wisdom:

"Don't be personal. Be dry! . . . Write in the third person as much as possible . . . No verifying! . . . Don't forget that few people are likely to tell more than a small part of the truth: no one tells much of the truth, let alone the whole truth . . . When people talk they reveal themselves, whether they're lying or telling the truth . . . Remember, any lie you are told, even deliberately, is often a more significant fact than a truth told in all sincerity. Don't correct them, and don't try to interpret them either."

What is this, if not a theory of spirituality and a theory of literature?

Obviously, the spiritual goings-on at Glacier have long since left Christianity behind. (Pastor Jón holds that all the gods people worship are equally good, that is, equally defective.) Clearly, there is much more than the order of nature. But is there any role for the gods—and religion? The impudent lightness with which the deep questions are raised in *Under the Glacier* is remote from the gravitas with which they figure in Russian and in German literature. This is a novel of immense charm that flirts with being a spoof. It is a satire on religion, full of amusing New Age mumbo-jumbo. It's a book of ideas, like no other Laxness ever wrote.

Laxness did not believe in the supernatural. Surely he

did believe in the cruelty of life—the laughter that is all that remains of the woman, Úa, to whom Embi had surrendered himself, and who has vanished. What transpired may seem like a dream, which is to say that the quest novel concludes with the obligatory return to reality. Embi is not to escape this morose destiny.

"Your emissary crept away with his duffel bag in the middle of the laughter," Embi concludes his report to the Bishop; so the novel ends. "I was a little frightened, and I ran as hard as I could back the way I had come. I was hoping that I would find the main road again."

Under the Glacier is a marvelous novel about the most ambitious questions, but since it is a novel, it is also a journey that must end, leaving the reader dazzled, provoked, and if Laxness's novel has done its job, perhaps not quite as eager as Embi to find the main road again.

. . .

9.11.01

To this appalled, sad American, and New Yorker, America has never seemed farther from an acknowledgment of reality than it's been in the face of last Tuesday's monstrous dose of reality. The disconnect between what happened and how it might be understood, and the self-righteous drivel and outright deceptions being peddled by virtually all our public figures (an exception: Mayor Giuliani) and TV commentators (an exception: Peter Jennings) is startling, depressing. The voices licensed to follow the event seem to have joined together in a campaign to infantilize the public. Where is the acknowledgment that this was not a "cowardly" attack on "civilization" or "liberty" or "humanity" or "the free world" but an attack on the world's self-proclaimed superpower, undertaken as a consequence of specific American alliances and actions? How many citizens are aware of the ongoing bombing of Iraq? And if the word "cowardly" is to be used, it might be more aptly applied to those who kill from beyond the range of retaliation, high in the sky, than to those willing to die themselves in order to kill others. In the matter of courage (a morally neutral virtue): whatever may be said of the perpetrators of Tuesday's slaughter, they were not cowards.

Our leaders are bent on convincing us that everything is okay. America is not afraid. "They" will be found and punished (whoever "they" may be). We have a robotic president who assures us that America still stands tall. A wide spectrum of public figures strongly opposed to the policies being pursued abroad by the Bush administration apparently feel free to say nothing more than that they stand, along with the whole American people, united and unafraid, behind President Bush. Commentators inform us that grief centers are in operation. Of course, we are not being shown any horrific images of what happened to the people working at the World Trade Center and the Pentagon. That might dispirit us. It was not until Thursday that public officials (again, with the exception of Mayor Giuliani) dared offer some estimates of the number of lives lost.

We have been told that everything is, or is going to be, okay, although this was a day that will live in infamy and America is now at war. But everything is not okay. And this was not Pearl Harbor. A lot of thinking needs to be done, and perhaps is being done in Washington and elsewhere, about the colossal failure of American intelligence and counter-intelligence, about the future of American foreign policy, particularly in the Middle East, and about what constitutes a sensible program of military defense. But clearly our leaders—those in public office, those aspiring to public office, those who once held public office—with the voluntary complicity of the principal media, have decided that the public is not to be asked to bear much of the burden of reality. The unanimously applauded, self-congratulatory bromides of a Soviet Party Congress seemed to us contemptible. The unanimity of the sanctimonious, reality-concealing rhetoric spouted by nearly all American officials and media commentators in these last days seems, well, unworthy of a mature democracy.

Our leaders have let us know that they consider their task to be a manipulative one: confidence-building and grief management. Politics, the politics of a democracy—which entails disagreement, which promotes candor—has been replaced by psychotherapy. Let's by all means grieve together. But let's not be stupid together. A few shreds of historical awareness might help us understand what has just happened, and what may continue to happen. "Our country is strong," we are told again and again. I for one don't find this entirely consoling. Who doubts that America is strong? But that's not all America has to be.

A Few Weeks After

1. Could you describe the impact of returning to New York? What did you feel when you saw the aftermath?

Of course, I would have preferred to have been in New York on September 11th. Because I was in Berlin, where I had gone for ten days, my initial reaction to what was taking place in the United States was, literally, mediated. Planning to spend all of that Tuesday afternoon writing in my silent room in a suburb of Berlin, abruptly alerted to what was happening in the middle of the morning in New York and Washington by phone calls from two friends, one in New York, the other in Bari, I rushed to turn on the TV and spent nearly all of the next forty-eight hours in front of the screen, mainly watching CNN, before returning to my laptop to dash off a diatribe against the inane and misleading demagoguery I had heard disseminated by American government and media figures.

(This short text, first published in *The New Yorker*, and fiercely criticized here in the United States, was of course only a first, but unfortunately all too accurate, impression.) Real grief followed in not altogether coherent stages, as it always does when one is removed from, and therefore deprived of full contact with, the reality of loss. Returning to New York late at night the following week, I drove directly from Kennedy Airport to as close as I could get by car to the site of the attack, and spent an hour prowling on foot around what is now a steaming, mountainous, foul-smelling mass graveyard—some six hectares large—in the southern part of Manhattan.

In those first days after my return to New York, the reality of the devastation, and the immensity of the loss of life, made my initial focus on the rhetoric surrounding the event seem to me less relevant. My consumption of reality via television had dropped to its usual level—zero. I have, stubbornly, never owned a TV set in America, although needless to say, I do watch TV when I am abroad. When I'm home, my principal sources of daily news are *The New York Times* as well as quite a few European papers I read online. And the *Times*, day after day, has published pages of heart-rending short biographies with pictures of many of the thousands of people who lost their lives in the hijacked airplanes and in the World Trade Center, including the more than three hundred firefighters who were racing up the stairs as the office workers were coming down. Among the dead were not only the well-paid, ambitious people who staffed the financial industries located there but many doing menial jobs in the buildings such as janitors, clerical assistants, and kitchen workers, more than seventy of them, mostly black and Hispanic, at Windows on the World, the restaurant at the top of one of the towers. So many stories; so many tears. To not mourn would be barbaric, just as it would be barbaric to think that these deaths are somehow different in kind from other atrocious losses of life, from Srebrenica to Rwanda.

But there is not only mourning to do. And so one does return to the discourse surrounding the event, and the reality of what has changed in America since September 11th.

2. What is your reaction to the rhetoric of Bush?

There is no reason to focus on the simplistic cowboy rhetoric of Bush, which, in the first days after September 11th, oscillated between the cretinous and the sinister—after which his speechwriters and advisers appear to have reined him in. Repulsive as were his demeanor and language, Bush should not monopolize our attention. All of the principal figures in the American government seem to me to be at a linguistic loss, as they search for images with which to encompass this unprecedented rebuke to American power and competence.

Two models for understanding the catastrophe of September 11th have been proposed. The first is that this is a war, initiated by a "sneak attack" comparable to the Japanese bombing of the U.S. naval base at Pearl Harbor, Hawaii, on December 7, 1941, which precipitated the Americans into World War II. The second, which has been gaining currency both in the United States and in Western Europe, is that this is a struggle between two rival civilizations, one productive, free, tolerant, and secular (or Christian), the other retrograde, bigoted, and vengeful.

Clearly, I am opposed to both of these vulgar, dangerous models for understanding what happened on September 11th. Not least among my reasons for rejecting both the "we are now at war" model and the "our civilization is superior to their civilization" model is that these views are exactly the views of those who perpetrated this criminal attack, and of the Wahhabi fundamentalist movement in Islam. If the American government persists in depicting this as a war, and satisfies the public's lust for the large-scale bombing campaign that Bush's rhetoric seemed to promise (at least at the beginning), the danger is likely to increase. It is not the terrorists who will suffer from an all-out "war" response on the part of the United States and its allies, but more innocent civilians—this time in Afghanistan, Iraq, and elsewhere—and these deaths can only inflame the hatred of the United States (and, more generally, of Western secularism) disseminated by radical Islamic fundamentalism.

Only violence that is very narrowly focused has a chance of reducing the threat posed by the movement of which Osama bin Laden is but one of many leaders. The situation seems to me extremely complicated. On the one hand, the activist terrorism that scored such a signal success on September 11th is clearly a global movement. It is not to be identified with a single state, certainly not just with wretched Afghanistan, as Pearl Harbor could be identified with Japan. Like today's economy, like the mass culture, like pandemic illness (think of AIDS), terrorism mocks borders. On the other hand, there are states that do figure at the center of the story. Saudi Arabia has provided the principal support worldwide for the Wahhabi movement (it is no accident that bin Laden is, in a manner of speaking, a Saudi prince), while during the same

period the Saudi monarchy has been America's most important ally in the Arab world. There are many among the
younger members of the Saudi elite besides bin Laden who regard the Saudi monarchy's cooperation with the United States
as a great "civilizational" betrayal. A full-scale American-led
"war" conducted against the terrorist movement identified
with bin Laden risks toppling the "reactionary" monarchy
and bringing the "radicals" to power in Saudi Arabia.

And this is only one of the many dilemmas facing the
U.S. policy-makers.

3. *You have stated that any comparison with Pearl Harbor
is inappropriate. As you know, Gore Vidal in his latest book,*
The Golden Age, *supports the thesis that Roosevelt provoked
the Japanese attack on Pearl Harbor to enable the United States
to enter the war alongside Britain and France. American public
opinion and Congress were against entering the war; only in the
case of attack could the United States have declared war. Some
other American intellectuals have joined Vidal in maintaining
that America has been provoking the Islamic world for years
and that, consequently, questioning U.S. policy is inevitable.
What is your opinion?*

As I've already suggested, I think that the comparison of
September 11th with Pearl Harbor is not only inappropriate
but misleading. It suggests that we have another nation to
contend with. The reality is that the forces seeking to humble
American power are, rather, subnational and transnational.
Osama bin Laden is, at most, the CEO of a vast conglomerate
of terror groups. Some informed people believe that he is even

a bit of a figurehead, valued more for his money and his charisma than for his operational talents. In this view, it is a core of Egyptian militants who are providing the real brains for an ongoing program of operations that may be expected to take place in many countries.

I have been a fervent critic of my country for almost as long as Gore Vidal, although I hope with more accuracy, and take for granted that questioning U.S. foreign policy is always desirable as well as inevitable. That being said, I don't believe that Roosevelt provoked the Japanese attack on Pearl Harbor. The Japanese government really was committed to the folly of starting a war with the United States. Neither do I think that America has been provoking the Islamic world for years. America has behaved brutally, imperially, in many countries, but it is not engaged in any overall operation against something that can be called "the Islamic world." And for all that I deplore about American foreign policy—and American imperial presumption and arrogance—the first thing to keep in mind is that what happened on September 11th was an appalling crime.

As someone who has been in the front line among those decrying American misdeeds for decades, I have been particularly outraged by, for example, the embargo that has brought so much suffering to the impoverished, oppressed people of Iraq. But the view I detect among some American intellectuals like Vidal and many *bien-pensant* intellectuals in Europe—that America has brought this horror upon itself, that America itself is, in part, to blame for the deaths of these thousands upon its own territory—is not, I repeat, not, a view that I share.

To in any way excuse or condone this atrocity by blaming the United States—even though there has been much in

American conduct abroad to blame—is morally obscene. Terrorism is the murder of innocent people. This time it was mass murder.

Further, I believe it is wrong to think of terrorism—this terrorism—as the pursuit of legitimate demands by illegitimate means. Let me be very specific. Were there to be tomorrow a unilateral withdrawal of Israel from the West Bank and Gaza followed, the day after, by the declaration of a Palestinian state accompanied by full guarantees of Israeli aid and cooperation, I believe that these altogether desirable events would make not even a dent in the terrorist projects currently under way. Terrorists cloak themselves in legitimate grievances, as Salman Rushdie has pointed out. The righting of these wrongs is not their purpose—only their shameless pretext.

What those who perpetrated the slaughter of September 11th were trying to achieve was not the righting of the wrongs done to the Palestinian people, or the suffering of people in most of the Muslim world. The attack was real. It was an attack on modernity (the only culture that makes possible the emancipation of women) and, yes, capitalism. And the modern world, our world, has been shown to be seriously vulnerable. An armed response—in the form of a complex and carefully focused set of counterterrorist operations; not a war—is necessary. And justified.

4. *Do you think public opinion in America, where a majority of the population doesn't bother to vote, can influence the decisions being taken by the government on how to respond to the attacks? How, if at all, has the intellectual climate changed in America since the attack?*

The United States is an odd country. Its citizens have a strong anarchic streak, and they also have an almost superstitious respect for legality. They worship amoral success, and they also love to moralize about right and wrong. They consider government and taxation to be deeply suspect, almost illegitimate, activities, but their most heartfelt response to any crisis is to wave their flag and affirm their unconditional love of country and approval of their leaders. Above all, they believe that America constitutes an exception in the course of human history and will always be exempt from the usual limitations and calamities that shape the destinies of other countries.

Right now there is a fiercely conformist mood in the United States. People were surprised and shocked by the success of the attack on September 11th. They are frightened. And the first response is to close ranks (to use the military image) and affirm their patriotism—as if that has been put in question by the attack. The country is swathed in American flags. The flags hang from the windows of apartments and houses, they drape the facades of stores and restaurants, they fly from cranes and trucks and car radio antennae. Mockery of the president—a traditional American pastime, no matter who the president—is thought to be unpatriotic. Journalists, a few, have been fired from newspapers and magazines. College teachers have been publicly reprimanded for voicing in their classrooms the mildest of critical observations (such as questioning Bush's mysterious disappearance on the day of the attack). Self-censorship, the most important and most successful form of censorship, is rampant. Debate is identified with dissent, which is in turn identified with disloyalty. There is a widespread feeling that, in this new, open-ended emergency, we may not be able to "afford" our traditional freedoms. Polls show Bush's "popularity ratings" to be running over ninety percent—a figure that comes close to the popularity of the leaders of the old Soviet-style dictatorships.

How could the opinions of the general public have any "influence" over the decisions being taken now by the American government? What is worth noting is how docile the public is about almost all matters of foreign policy. This passivity may be an inevitable consequence of the triumph of liberal capitalism and the consumer society. For some time there has ceased to be any significant difference between the Democrats and the Republicans; they are best thought of as two branches of the same party. (A similar evolution is to be observed in Great Britain, where there is now hardly any difference between the Labor and Conservative parties.) The depoliticization of most of the American intelligentsia merely reflects the conformism and convergence—the "me-tooism"—of political life in general.

America is a notably tolerant society as well as a conformist one; that is the paradox of the political culture that has been constructed here. But should there be another terrorist attack within the borders of the United States in the near future, even one that causes a relatively small loss of life, the damage to the wide support of heterodoxy and diversity could be permanent. Something like martial law could be imposed, which would entail the collapse of the constitutional protections of individual rights, particularly of freedom of speech. For the moment, however, I remain guardedly optimistic. Some of the current furor of vindictiveness against dissenting intellectuals like myself—and we are, alas, few—

may soon dissipate as people are obliged to worry about real problems, such as the failing economy.

Right now we hear hardly any cowboy talk from the Bush administration, following what must have been, since September 11th, some very strenuous debates in the highest government-military circles. Clearly, our masters of war have realized that we face an exceedingly complex "enemy" who cannot be defeated by the old means. That there has been hesitation about what action to take owes nothing to American public opinion, which has been prepared for swift punishment.

One can only hope that something intelligent is being planned to make our populations safer from the jihad against modernity. And one can only hope that the Bush administration, Tony Blair, et al. have really understood that it would be useless or, as they say, counterproductive—as well as wicked—to bomb the oppressed people of Afghanistan and Iraq and elsewhere in retaliation for the misdeeds of their tyrants and reigning religious lunatics. One can only hope . . .

One Year After

Since last September 11th, the Bush administration has told the American people, America is now at war. But this war has a rather peculiar nature. It seems to be, given the nature of the enemy, a war with no foreseeable end. What kind of war is that?

There are precedents. Wars declared in recent years on such enemies as cancer, poverty, and drugs are understood to be endless wars. As everyone knows, there will always be cancer, poverty, and drugs. And there will always be despicable terrorists, terrorists who are mass murderers, such as those who perpetrated the attack last September 11th, as well as freedom fighters once called terrorists (as was the French Resistance by the Vichy government, and the ANC and Nelson Mandela by the apartheid South African government) but subsequently relabeled by history.

When a president of the United States declares war on cancer or poverty or drugs, we know that "war" is a metaphor.

Does anyone think that this war—the war that America has declared on terrorism—is a metaphor? But it is, and one with powerful consequences. The war has been disclosed, not actually declared, since the threat is deemed to be self-evident.

Real wars are not metaphors. And real wars have a beginning and an end. Even the horrendous, intractable conflict between Israel and Palestine will end one day. But the war that has been decreed by the Bush administration will never end. That is one sign that it is not a war but, rather, a mandate for expanding the use of American power.

When the government declares war on cancer or poverty or drugs, it means the government is asking that new forces be mobilized to address the problem. It also means that the government is not going to do a whole lot to solve it. When the government declares war on terrorism—terrorism being a multinational, largely clandestine network of enemies—it means that the government can do what it wants. When it wants to intervene somewhere, it will. It will brook no limits on its power.

The American suspicion of foreign "entanglements" is very old. But this administration has taken the radical position that *all* international treaties are potentially inimical to the interests of the United States—since by signing a treaty on anything (say, environmental issues, or the conduct of war and the treatment of prisoners, or a world court), the United States is binding itself to obey conventions that might one day be invoked to limit America's freedom of action to do whatever the government thinks is in the country's interests. Indeed, that's what a treaty is: it limits the right of its signatories to complete freedom of action on the subject of the treaty. It has not up to now been the avowed position of any respectable nation-state that this is a reason for eschewing treaties.

Describing America's new foreign policy as actions undertaken in wartime is a powerful disincentive to having a mainstream debate about what is actually happening. This reluctance to ask questions was already apparent in the immediate aftermath of the attacks last September 11th. Those who objected to the jihad language used by the American government (good versus evil, civilization versus barbarism) were accused of condoning the attacks, or at least the legitimacy of the grievances behind the attacks.

Under the slogan "United We Stand," the call to reflection was equated with dissent, dissent with lack of patriotism. The indignation suited those who have taken charge of the Bush administration's foreign policy. The aversion to debate among the principal figures in the two parties continues to be apparent in the run-up to the commemorative ceremonies on the anniversary of the attacks—ceremonies that are viewed as the continuing affirmation of American solidarity against the enemy.

The comparison between September 11, 2001, and December 7, 1941, has never been far from mind. Once again America was the object of a lethal surprise attack that cost many—in this case, civilian—lives, more than the number of soldiers and sailors who died at Pearl Harbor. However, I doubt that great commemorative ceremonies were felt to be needed to keep up morale and unite the country on December 7, 1942. That was a real war and one year later was still going on.

This is a phantom war, a war at the pleasure of the Bush administration, and therefore in need of an anniversary. Such an anniversary serves a number of purposes. It is a day of mourning. It is an affirmation of national solidarity. But of one thing we can be sure. It is not a day of national reflection. Reflection, it has been said, might impair our "moral clarity." It is necessary to be simple, clear, united. Hence there will be no words; rather, there will be borrowed words, like the Gettysburg Address (claimed by both political parties), from that bygone era when great rhetoric was possible. But Abraham Lincoln's speeches were not just inspirational prose. They were bold statements of new national goals in a time of real, terrible war. The Second Inaugural Address dared to herald the reconciliation between North and South that must follow Northern victory in the Civil War. The primacy of the commitment to end slavery was the point of the exaltation of freedom in the Gettysburg Address. When the great Lincoln speeches are cited at the commemorative ceremonies of September 11th, they have—in true postmodernist fashion— become completely emptied of meaning. They are now gestures of nobility, of greatness of spirit. What they were being great about is irrelevant.

It is all in the grand tradition of American anti-intellectualism: the suspicion of thought, of words. And it very much serves the purposes of the present administration. Hiding behind the humbug that the attack of last September 11th was too horrible, too devastating, too painful, too tragic for words, that words could not possibly do justice to our grief and indignation, our leaders have a perfect excuse to drape themselves in borrowed words voided of content. To say something might be controversial. It might actually drift into some kind of statement and therefore invite rebuttal. Not saying anything is best.

Of course, there will be pictures. Lots of pictures. As old words will be recycled, so will the pictures of a year ago. A picture, as everyone knows, is worth a thousand words. We will relive the event. There will be interviews with survivors and with the members of the families of those who died in the attacks. It's closure time in the gardens of the West. (I used to think the piece of verbal flummery that represented the great current threat to seriousness and to justice was "elitist." I've come to regard "closure" as just as phony and odious.) Some will get closure, others will refuse it, needing to continue with the mourning. City officials will read aloud the names of those who died in the Twin Towers—an oral version of the most admired monument of mourning in the United States, Maya Lin's interactive black stone screen in Washington, D.C., on which is incised (for reading, for touching) the name of every single American who died in Vietnam. Other bits of linguistic magic will follow, such as the decision just announced that the international airport across the river in New Jersey, from where United 93 took off on its doomed flight, will henceforth be called Newark Liberty Airport.

Let me be even clearer. I do not question that there is a vicious, abhorrent enemy that opposes most of what I cherish—including democracy, pluralism, secularism, the absolute equality of the sexes, beardless men, dancing (all kinds), skimpy clothing, and, well, fun. Not for a moment do I question the obligation of the American government, as of any government, to protect the lives of its citizens. What I do question is the pseudo-declaration of pseudo-war. These necessary actions should not be called a "war." There are no endless wars. But there are declarations of the extension of power by a state that believes it cannot be challenged.

America has every right to hunt down the perpetrators of these crimes and their accomplices. But this determination is not necessarily a war. Limited, focused military engagements abroad do not translate into "wartime" at home. There are better ways to check America's enemies, less destructive of constitutional rights and of international agreements that serve the public interest of all, than continuing to invoke the dangerous, lobotomizing notion of endless war.

Photography:
A Little Summa

1. Photography is, first of all, a way of seeing. It is not seeing itself.

2. It is the ineluctably "modern" way of seeing— prejudiced in favor of projects of discovery and innovation.

3. This way of seeing, which now has a long history, shapes what we look for and are used to noticing in photographs.

4. The modern way of seeing is to see in fragments. It is felt that reality is essentially unlimited, and knowledge is open-ended. It follows that all boundaries, all unifying ideas have to be misleading, demagogic; at best, provisional; almost always, in the long run, untrue. To see reality in the light of certain unifying ideas has the undeniable advantage of giving

shape and form to our experience. But it also—so the modern way of seeing instructs us—denies the infinite variety and complexity of the real. Thereby it represses our energy, indeed our right, to remake what we wish to remake—our society, our selves. What is liberating, we are told, is to notice more and more.

5. In a modern society, images made by cameras are the principal access to realities of which we have no direct experience. And we are expected to receive and to register an unlimited number of images of what we don't directly experience. The camera defines for us what we allow to be "real"—and it continually pushes forward the boundary of the real. Photographers are particularly admired if they reveal hidden truths about themselves or less than fully reported social conflicts in societies both near and far from where the viewer lives.

6. In the modern way of knowing, there have to be images for something to become "real." Photographs identify events. Photographs confer importance on events and make them memorable. For a war, an atrocity, a pandemic, a so-called natural disaster to become a subject of large concern, it has to reach people through the various systems (from television and the internet to newspapers and magazines) that diffuse photographic images to millions.

7. In the modern way of seeing, reality is first of all appearance—which is always changing. A photograph records appearance. The record of photography is the record of change, of the destruction of the past. Being modern (and if we have the habit of looking at photographs, we are by definition

modern), we understand all identities to be constructions. The only irrefutable reality—and our best clue to identity— is how people appear.

8. A photograph is a fragment—a glimpse. We accumulate glimpses, fragments. All of us mentally stock hundreds of photographic images, subject to instant recall. All photographs aspire to the condition of being memorable—that is, unforgettable.

9. In the view that defines us as modern, there are an infinite number of details. Photographs are details. Therefore, photographs seem like life. To be modern is to live, entranced, by the savage autonomy of the detail.

10. To know is, first of all, to acknowledge. Recognition is the form of knowledge that is now identified with art. The photographs of the terrible cruelties and injustices that afflict most people in the world seem to be telling us—we who are privileged and relatively safe—that we should be aroused; that we should want something done to stop these horrors. And then there are photographs that seem to invite a different kind of attention. For this ongoing body of work, photography is not a species of social or moral agitation, meant to prod us to feel and to act, but an enterprise of notation. We watch, we take note, we acknowledge. This is a cooler way of looking. This is the way of looking we identify as art.

11. The work of some of the best socially engaged photographers is often reproached if it seems too much like art. And photography understood as art may incur a parallel reproach—

that it deadens concern. It shows us events and situations and conflicts that we might deplore, and asks us to be detached. It may show us something truly horrifying and be a test of what we can bear to look at and are supposed to accept. Or often— this is true of a good deal of the most brilliant contemporary photography—it simply invites us to stare at banality. To stare at banality and also to relish it, drawing on the very developed habits of irony that are affirmed by the surreal juxtapositions of photographs typical of sophisticated exhibitions and books.

12. Photography—the supreme form of travel, of tourism—is the principal modern means for enlarging the world. As a branch of art, photography's enterprise of world-enlargement tends to specialize in the subjects felt to be challenging, transgressive. A photograph may be telling us: this too exists. And that. And that. (And it is all "human.") But what are we to do with this knowledge—if indeed it is knowledge, about, say, the self, about abnormality, about ostracized or clandestine worlds?

13. Call it knowledge, call it acknowledgment—of one thing we can be sure, about this distinctively modern way of experiencing anything: the seeing, and the accumulation of fragments of seeing, can never be completed.

14. There is no final photograph.

Regarding the Torture
of Others

For a long time—at least six decades—photographs have laid down the tracks of how important conflicts are judged and remembered. The Western memory museum is now mostly a visual one. Photographs have an insuperable power to determine what we recall of events, and it now seems probable that the defining association of people everywhere with the rotten war that the United States launched preemptively in Iraq last year will be photographs of the torture of Iraqi prisoners by Americans in the most infamous of Saddam Hussein's prisons, Abu Ghraib.

The Bush administration and its defenders have chiefly sought to limit a public relations disaster—the dissemination of the photographs—rather than deal with the complex crimes of leadership and of policy revealed by the pictures. There was, first of all, the displacement of the reality onto the photographs themselves. The administration's initial response was to say that the president was shocked and disgusted by the photographs—as if the fault or horror lay in the images, not in what they depict. There was also the avoidance of the word "torture." The prisoners had possibly been the objects of "abuse," eventually of "humiliation"—that was the most to be admitted. "My impression is that what has been charged thus far is abuse, which I believe technically is different from torture," Secretary of Defense Donald Rumsfeld said at a press conference. "And therefore I'm not going to address the 'torture' word."

Words alter, words add, words subtract. It was the strenuous avoidance of the word "genocide" while some 800,000 Tutsis in Rwanda were being slaughtered, over a few weeks' time, by their Hutu neighbors ten years ago that indicated the American government had no intention of doing anything. To refuse to call what took place in Abu Ghraib—and what has taken place elsewhere in Iraq and in Afghanistan and at Guantánamo Bay—by its true name, torture, is as outrageous as the refusal to call the Rwandan genocide a genocide. Here is one of the definitions of torture contained in a convention to which the United States is a signatory: "any act by which severe pain or suffering, whether physical or mental, is intentionally inflicted on a person for such purposes as obtaining from him or a third person information or a confession." (The definition comes from the 1984 Convention Against Torture and Other Cruel, Inhuman or Degrading Treatment or Punishment. Similar definitions have existed for some time in customary law and in treaties, starting with Article 3—common to the four Geneva Conventions of 1949—and many recent human rights conventions.) The 1984 convention declares: "No exceptional circumstances what-

soever, whether a state of war or a threat of war, internal political instability or any other public emergency, may be invoked
as a justification of torture." And all covenants on torture
specify that it includes treatment intended to humiliate the
victim, like leaving prisoners naked in cells and corridors.

Whatever actions this administration undertakes to
limit the damage of the widening revelations of the torture
of prisoners in Abu Ghraib and elsewhere—trials, courts-
martial, dishonorable discharges, resignation of senior military
figures and responsible administration officials, and substantial compensation to the victims—it is probable that the "torture" word will continue to be banned. To acknowledge that
Americans torture their prisoners would contradict everything
this administration has invited the public to believe about the
virtue of American intentions and the universality of American values, which is the ultimate, triumphalist justification of
America's right to unilateral action on the world stage in defense of its interests and its security.

Even when the president was finally compelled, as the
damage to America's reputation everywhere in the world
widened and deepened, to use the "sorry" word, the focus of
regret still seemed the damage to America's claim to moral
superiority, to its hegemonic goal of bringing "freedom and
democracy" to the benighted Middle East. Yes, Mr. Bush said
in Washington on May 6, standing alongside King Abdullah
II of Jordan, he was "sorry for the humiliation suffered by the
Iraqi prisoners and the humiliation suffered by their families." But, he went on, he was "equally sorry that people who
have been seeing those pictures didn't understand the true
nature and heart of America."

To have the American effort in Iraq summed up by these

images must seem, to those who saw some justification in a war that did overthrow one of the monster tyrants of modern times, "unfair." A war, an occupation, is inevitably a huge tapestry of actions. What makes some actions representative and others not? The issue is not whether the torture was done by individuals (i.e., "not by everybody") but whether it was systematic. Authorized. Condoned. All acts are done by individuals. The issue is not whether a majority or a minority of Americans performs such acts but whether the nature of the policies prosecuted by this administration and the hierarchies deployed to carry them out makes such acts likely.

·

Considered in this light, the photographs *are* us. That is, they are representative of the fundamental corruptions of any foreign occupation together with the Bush administration's distinctive policies. The Belgians in the Congo, the French in Algeria, practiced torture and sexual humiliation on despised recalcitrant natives. Add to this generic corruption the mystifying, near-total unpreparedness of the American rulers of Iraq to deal with the complex realities of the country after its "liberation"—that is, conquest. And add to that the overarching doctrines of the Bush administration, namely that the United States has embarked on an endless war (against a protean enemy called "terrorism") and that those detained in this war are, if the president so decides, "unlawful combatants"—a policy enunciated by Donald Rumsfeld as early as January 2002—and thus, as Rumsfeld said, "technically" they "do not have any rights under the Geneva Convention," and you have a perfect recipe for the cruelties and crimes committed against the thousands incarcerated without charges or access to lawyers in American-run prisons that have been set up since the attacks of September 11, 2001.

So then, is the real issue not the photographs themselves but what the photographs reveal to have happened to "suspects" in American custody? No: the horror of what is shown in the photographs cannot be separated from the horror that the photographs were taken—with the perpetrators posing, gloating, over their helpless captives. German soldiers in the Second World War took photographs of the atrocities they were committing in Poland and Russia, but snapshots in which the executioners placed themselves among their victims are exceedingly rare, as may be seen in *Photographing the Holocaust* by Janina Struk. If there is something comparable to what these pictures show, it would be some of the photographs of black victims of lynching taken between the 1880s and 1930s, which show Americans grinning beneath the naked mutilated body of a black man or woman hanging behind them from a tree. The lynching photographs were souvenirs of a collective action whose participants felt perfectly justified in what they had done. So are the pictures from Abu Ghraib.

If there is a difference, it is a difference created by the increasing ubiquity of photographic actions. The lynching pictures were in the nature of photographs as trophies— taken by a photographer, in order to be collected, stored in albums, displayed. The pictures taken by American soldiers in Abu Ghraib, however, reflect a shift in the use made of pictures—less objects to be saved than messages to be disseminated, circulated. A digital camera is a common possession among soldiers. Where once photographing war was the province of photojournalists, now the soldiers themselves are all photographers—recording their war, their fun, their observations of what they find picturesque, their atrocities—and swapping images among themselves, and e-mailing them around the globe.

There is more and more recording of what people do, by themselves. At least or especially in America, Andy Warhol's ideal of filming real events in real time—life isn't edited, why should its record be edited?—has become a norm for countless webcasts, in which people record their day, each in his or her own reality show. Here I am—waking and yawning and stretching, brushing my teeth, making breakfast, getting the kids off to school. People record all aspects of their lives, store them in computer files, and send the files around. Family life goes with the recording of family life—even when, or especially when, the family is in the throes of crisis and disgrace. Surely the dedicated, incessant home-videoing of one another, in conversation and monologue, over many years was the most astonishing material in *Capturing the Friedmans* (2003), Andrew Jarecki's documentary about a Long Island family embroiled in pedophilia charges.

An erotic life is, for more and more people, that which can be captured in digital photographs and on video. And perhaps the torture is more attractive, as something to record, when it has a sexual component. It is surely revealing, as more Abu Ghraib photographs enter public view, that torture photographs are interleaved with pornographic images of American soldiers having sex with one another. In fact, most of the torture photographs have a sexual theme, as in those showing the coercing of prisoners to perform, or simulate, sexual acts among themselves. One exception, already canonical, is the photo-

graph of the man made to stand on a box, hooded and sprout-
ing wires, reportedly told he would be electrocuted if he fell
off. Yet pictures of prisoners bound in painful positions, or
made to stand with outstretched arms, are infrequent. That
they count as torture cannot be doubted. You have only to look
at the terror on the victim's face. But most of the pictures seem
part of a larger confluence of torture and pornography: a young
woman leading a naked man around on a leash is classic dom-
inatrix imagery. And you wonder how much of the sexual tor-
tures inflicted on the inmates of Abu Ghraib was inspired by
the vast repertory of pornographic imagery available on the
internet—and which ordinary people, by sending out webcasts themselves, try to emulate.

·

To live is to be photographed, to have a record of one's
life, and therefore to go on with one's life oblivious, or claiming to be oblivious, to the camera's nonstop attentions. But to
live is also to pose. To act is to share in the community of actions recorded as images. The expression of satisfaction at the
acts of torture being inflicted on helpless, trussed, naked victims is only part of the story. There is the deep satisfaction of
being photographed, to which one is now more inclined to
respond not with a stiff, direct gaze (as in former times) but
with glee. The events are in part designed to be photographed.
The grin is a grin for the camera. There would be something
missing if, after stacking the naked men, you couldn't take a
picture of them.

Looking at these photographs, you ask yourself, how can
someone grin at the sufferings and humiliation of another
human being? Set guard dogs at the genitals and legs of cow-

ering naked prisoners? Force shackled, hooded prisoners to masturbate or simulate oral sex with one another? And you feel naïve for asking, since the answer is, self-evidently, people do these things to other people. Rape and pain inflicted on the genitals are among the most common forms of torture. Not just in Nazi concentration camps and in Abu Ghraib when it was run by Saddam Hussein. Americans too have done and do them when they are told, or made to feel, that those over whom they have absolute power deserve to be humiliated, tormented. They do them when they are led to believe that the people they are torturing belong to an inferior race or religion. For the meaning of these pictures is not just that these acts were performed but that their perpetrators apparently had no sense that there was anything wrong in what the pictures show.

Even more appalling, since the pictures were meant to be circulated and seen by many people: it was all fun. And this idea of fun is, alas, more and more—contrary to what Mr. Bush is telling the world—part of "the true nature and heart of America." It is hard to measure the increasing acceptance of brutality in American life, but its evidence is everywhere, starting with the video games of killing that are a principal entertainment of boys—can the video game *Interrogating the Terrorists* really be far behind?—and on to the violence that has become endemic in the group rites of youth on an exuberant kick. Violent crime is down, yet the easy delight taken in violence seems to have grown. From the harsh torments inflicted on incoming students in many American suburban high schools—depicted in Richard Linklater's film *Dazed and Confused* (1993)—to the hazing rituals of physical brutality and sexual humiliation in college fraternities and on sports teams, America has become a country in which the fantasies and the practice of violence are seen as good entertainment, fun.

What formerly was segregated as pornography, as the exercise of extreme sadomasochistic longings—as in Pier Paolo Pasolini's last, near-unwatchable film, *Salò* (1975), depicting orgies of torture in the Fascist redoubt in northern Italy at the end of the Mussolini era—is now being normalized, by the apostles of the new, bellicose, imperial America, as high-spirited prankishness or venting. To "stack naked men" is like a college fraternity prank, said a caller to Rush Limbaugh and the many millions of Americans who listen to his radio show. Had the caller, one wonders, seen the photographs? No matter. The observation—or is it the fantasy?—was on the mark. What may still be capable of shocking some Americans was Limbaugh's response: "Exactly!" he exclaimed. "Exactly my point. This is no different than what happens at the Skull and Bones initiation, and we're going to ruin people's lives over it, and we're going to hamper our military effort, and then we are going to really hammer them because they had a good time." "They" are the American soldiers, the torturers. And Limbaugh went on: "You know, these people are being fired at every day. I'm talking about people having a good time, these people. You ever heard of emotional release?"

It's likely that quite a large number of Americans would rather think that it is all right to torture and humiliate other human beings—who, as our putative or suspected enemies, have forfeited all their rights—than to acknowledge the folly and ineptitude and fraud of the American venture in Iraq. As for torture and sexual humiliation as fun, there seems little to oppose this tendency while America continues to turn itself into a garrison state, in which patriots are defined as those with unconditional respect for armed might and the necessity of maximal domestic surveillance. Shock and awe were what our military promised the Iraqis. And shock and the awful are what these photographs announce to the world that the Americans have delivered: a pattern of criminal behavior in open contempt of international humanitarian conventions. Soldiers now pose, thumbs up, before the atrocities they commit, and send off the pictures to their buddies. Should we be entirely surprised? Ours is a society in which secrets of private life that, formerly, you would have given nearly anything to conceal, you now clamor to be invited on a television show to reveal. What is illustrated by these photographs is as much the culture of shamelessness as the reigning admiration for unapologetic brutality.

·

The notion that apologies or professions of "disgust" by the president and the secretary of defense are a sufficient response is an insult to one's historical and moral sense. The torture of prisoners is not an aberration. It is a direct consequence of the with-us-or-against-us doctrines of world struggle with which the Bush administration has sought to change, change radically, the international stance of the United States and to recast many domestic institutions and prerogatives. The Bush administration has committed the country to a pseudo-religious doctrine of war, endless war—for "the war on terror" is nothing less than that. What has happened in the new, international carceral empire run by the United States military goes beyond even the notorious procedures in France's

Devil's Island and Soviet Russia's Gulag system, which in the case of the French penal island had, first, both trials and sentences, and in the case of the Russian prison empire a charge of some kind and a sentence for a specific number of years. Endless war is taken to justify endless incarcerations. Those held in the extralegal American penal empire are "detainees"; "prisoners," a newly obsolete word, might suggest that they have the rights accorded by international law and the laws of all civilized countries. This endless "global war on terrorism"—into which both the quite justified invasion of Afghanistan and the unwinnable folly in Iraq have been folded by Pentagon decree—inevitably leads to the demonizing and dehumanizing of anyone declared by the Bush administration to be a possible terrorist: a definition that is not up for debate and is, in fact, usually made in secret.

The charges against most of the people detained in the prisons in Iraq and Afghanistan being nonexistent—the Red Cross reports that seventy to ninety percent of those being held seem to have committed no crime other than simply being in the wrong place at the wrong time, caught up in some sweep of "suspects"—the principal justification for holding them is "interrogation." Interrogation about what? About anything. Whatever the detainee might know. If interrogation is the point of detaining prisoners indefinitely, then physical coercion, humiliation, and torture become inevitable.

Remember: we are not talking about that rarest of cases, the "ticking time-bomb" situation, which is sometimes used as a limiting case that justifies torture of prisoners who have knowledge of an imminent attack. This is general or nonspecific information-gathering, authorized by American military and civilian administrators to learn more of a shadowy empire of evildoers about which Americans know virtually nothing, in countries about whom they are singularly ignorant: in principle, any information at all might be useful. An interrogation that produced no information (whatever information might consist of) would count as a failure. All the more justification for preparing prisoners to talk. Softening them up, stressing them out—these are the euphemisms for the bestial practices in American prisons where suspected terrorists are being held. Unfortunately, it seems, more than a few got too stressed out and died.

The pictures will not go away. That is the nature of the digital world in which we live. Indeed, it seems they were necessary to get our leaders to acknowledge that they had a problem on their hands. After all, the conclusions of reports compiled by the International Committee of the Red Cross, and other reports by journalists and protests by humanitarian organizations about the atrocious punishments inflicted on "detainees" and "suspected terrorists" in prisons run by the American military, first in Afghanistan and later in Iraq, have been circulating for more than a year. It seems doubtful that such reports were read by Mr. Bush or Mr. Cheney or Ms. Rice or Mr. Rumsfeld. Apparently it took the photographs to get their attention, when it became clear they could not be suppressed; it was the photographs that made all this "real" to the president and his associates. Up to then there had been only words, which are easier to cover up in our age of infinite digital self-reproduction and self-dissemination, and so much easier to forget.

So now the pictures will continue to "assault" us—as many Americans are bound to feel. Will people get used to them? Some Americans are already saying they have seen

enough. Not, however, the rest of the world. Endless war: endless stream of photographs. Will editors now debate whether
showing more of them, or showing them uncropped (which,
with some of the best-known images, like that of a hooded
man on a box, gives a different and in some instances more
appalling view), would be in "bad taste" or too implicitly political? By "political," read: critical of the Bush administration's imperial project. For there can be no doubt that the
photographs damage, as Mr. Rumsfeld testified, "the reputation of the honorable men and women of the armed forces
who are courageously and responsibly and professionally defending our freedom across the globe." This damage—to our
reputation, our image, our success as the lone superpower—is
what the Bush administration principally deplores. How the
protection of "our freedom"—the freedom of five percent of
humanity—came to require having American soldiers across
the globe is hardly debated by our elected officials. America
sees itself as the victim of potential or future terror. America
is only defending itself, against implacable, furtive enemies.

Already the backlash has begun. Americans are being
warned against indulging in an orgy of self-condemnation.
The continuing publication of the pictures is being taken by
many Americans as suggesting that we do not have the right to
defend ourselves: after all, they (the terrorists) started it.
They—Osama bin Laden? Saddam Hussein? what's the difference?—attacked us first. James Inhofe of Oklahoma, a Republican member of the Senate Armed Services Committee,
before which Secretary Rumsfeld testified, avowed that he was
sure he was not the only member of the committee "more outraged by the outrage" over the photographs than by what the
photographs showed. "These prisoners," Senator Inhofe ex-

plained, "you know, they're not there for traffic violations. If they're in Cellblock 1-A or 1-B, these prisoners, they're murderers, they're terrorists, they're insurgents. Many of them probably have American blood on their hands, and here we're so concerned about the treatment of those individuals." It's the fault of "the media," which are provoking, and will continue to provoke, further violence against Americans around the world. More Americans will die. Because of these photos.

It would be a great mistake to let these revelations of the American military and civilian authorization of torture in the "global war against terrorism" become a story of the war of—and against—the images. Americans are dying not because of the photographs but because of what the photographs reveal to be happening, happening at the behest of and with the complicity of a chain of command that reaches up to the highest level of the Bush administration. But the distinction between photograph and reality—as between spin and policy—can easily evaporate. And that is what the administration wishes to happen.

"There are a lot more photographs and videos that exist," Mr. Rumsfeld acknowledged in his testimony. "If these are released to the public, obviously it's going to make matters worse." Worse for the administration and its programs, presumably, not for those who are the actual—and potential—victims of torture.

The media may self-censor, but as Mr. Rumsfeld acknowledged, it's hard to censor soldiers overseas, who don't write letters home, as in the old days, that can be opened by military censors who ink out unacceptable lines. Today's soldiers instead function like tourists, as Mr. Rumsfeld put it, "running around with digital cameras and taking these unbelievable photographs and then passing them off, against the law, to the media, to our surprise." The administration's effort to withhold pictures is proceeding along several fronts. Currently, the argument is taking a legalistic turn: now the photographs are classified as evidence in future criminal cases, whose outcome may be prejudiced if they are made public. The Republican chairman of the Senate Armed Services Committee, John Warner of Virginia, after the May 12 slide show of image after image of sexual humiliation and violence against Iraqi prisoners, said he felt "very strongly" that the newer photos "should not be made public. I feel that it could possibly endanger the men and women of the armed forces as they are serving and at great risk."

But the real push to limit the accessibility of the photographs will come from the continuing effort to protect the administration and cover up our misrule in Iraq—to identify "outrage" over the photographs with a campaign to undermine American military might and the purposes it currently serves. Just as it was regarded by many as an implicit criticism of the war to show on television photographs of American soldiers who have been killed in the course of the invasion and occupation of Iraq, it will increasingly be thought unpatriotic to disseminate the new photographs and further tarnish the image of America.

After all, we're at war. Endless war. And war is hell, more so than any of the people who got us into this rotten war seem to have expected. In our digital hall of mirrors, the pictures aren't going to go away. Yes, it seems that one picture is worth a thousand words. And even if our leaders choose not to look at them, there will be thousands more snapshots and videos. Unstoppable.

The Conscience of Words

The Jerusalem Prize Acceptance Speech

We fret about words, we writers. Words mean. Words point. They are arrows. Arrows stuck in the rough hide of reality. And the more portentous, more general the word, the more they also resemble rooms or tunnels. They can expand, or cave in. They can come to be filled with a bad smell. They will often remind us of other rooms, where we'd rather dwell or where we think we are already living. They can be spaces we lose the art or the wisdom of inhabiting. And eventually those volumes of mental intention we no longer know how to in- habit will be abandoned, boarded up, closed down.

What do we mean, for example, by the word "peace"? Do we mean an absence of strife? Do we mean a forgetting? Do we mean a forgiveness? Or do we mean a great weariness, an exhaustion, an emptying out of rancor?

It seems to me that what most people mean by "peace"

is victory. The victory of *their* side. That's what "peace" means to *them*, while to the others peace means defeat.

If the idea takes hold that peace, while in principle to be desired, entails an unacceptable renunciation of legitimate claims, then the most plausible course will be the practice of war by less than total means. Calls for peace will be felt to be, if not fraudulent, then certainly premature. Peace becomes a space people no longer know how to inhabit. Peace has to be re-settled. Re-colonized . . .

.

And what do we mean by "honor"?

Honor as an exacting standard of private conduct seems to belong to some faraway time. But the custom of conferring honors—to flatter ourselves and one another—continues unabated.

To confer an honor is to affirm a standard believed to be held in common. To accept an honor is to believe, for a moment, that one has deserved it. (The most one should say, in all decency, is that one is not *un*worthy of it.) To refuse an honor offered seems boorish, unconvivial, pretentious.

A prize accumulates honor—and the ability to confer honor—by the choice it has made in previous years of whom to honor.

By this standard, consider the polemically named Jerusalem Prize, which, in its relatively short history, has been awarded to some of the best writers of the second half of the twentieth century. Though by any obvious criteria a literary prize, it is not called The Jerusalem Prize for Literature but The Jerusalem Prize for the Freedom of the Individual in Society.

· · ·

Have all the writers who have won the prize really championed the Freedom of the Individual in Society? Is *that* what they—now I must say "we"—have in common?

I think not.

Not only do they represent a large spectrum of political opinion. Some of them have barely touched the Big Words: freedom, individual, society . . .

But it isn't what a writer says that matters, it's what a writer *is*.

Writers—by which I mean members of the community of literature—are emblems of the persistence (and the necessity) of individual vision.

I prefer to use "individual" as an adjective rather than as a noun.

The unceasing propaganda in our time for "the individual" seems to me deeply suspect, as "individuality" itself becomes more and more a synonym for selfishness. A capitalist society comes to have a vested interest in praising "individuality" and "freedom"—which may mean little more than the right to the perpetual aggrandizement of the self, and the freedom to shop, to acquire, to use up, to consume, to render obsolete.

I don't believe there is any inherent value in the cultivation of the self. And I think there is no culture (using the term normatively) without a standard of altruism, of regard for others. I do believe there is an inherent value in extending our sense of what a human life can be. If literature has engaged me as a project, first as a reader and then as a writer, it is as an extension of my sympathies to other selves, other domains, other dreams, other words, other territories of concern.

·

As a writer, a maker of literature, I am both a narrator and a ruminator. Ideas move me. But novels are made not of ideas but of forms. Forms of language. Forms of expressiveness. I don't have a story in my head until I have the form. (As Vladimir Nabokov said: "The pattern of the thing precedes the thing.") And—implicitly or tacitly—novels are made out of the writer's sense of what literature is or can be.

Every writer's work, every literary performance is, or amounts to, an account of literature itself. The defense of literature has become one of the writer's main subjects. But as Oscar Wilde observed, "A truth in art is that whose contradictory is also true." Paraphrasing Wilde, I would say: A truth about literature is that whose opposite is also true.

Thus, literature—and I speak prescriptively, not just descriptively—is self-consciousness, doubt, scruple, fastidiousness. It is also—again, prescriptively as well as descriptively— song, spontaneity, celebration, bliss.

Ideas about literature—unlike ideas about, say, love— almost never arise except in response to other people's ideas. They are reactive ideas.

I say *this* because it's my impression that you—or most people—are saying *that*.

Thereby I want to make room for a larger passion or different practice. Ideas give permission—and I want to give permission to a different feeling or practice.

I say this when you're saying that, not just because writers are, sometimes, professional adversaries. Not just to redress the inevitable imbalance or one-sidedness of any practice which has the character of an institution—and literature *is* an institution—but because literature is a practice which is rooted in inherently contradictory aspirations.

My view is that any one account of literature is untrue—that is, reductive; merely polemical. While to speak truthfully about literature is necessarily to speak in paradoxes.

Thus, each work of literature that matters, that deserves the name of literature, incarnates an ideal of singularity, of the singular voice. But literature, which is an accumulation, incarnates an ideal of plurality, of multiplicity, of promiscuity.

Every notion of literature we can think of—literature as social engagement, literature as the pursuit of private spiritual intensities, national literature, world literature—is, or can become, a form of spiritual complacency, or vanity, or self-congratulation.

Literature is a system—a plural system—of standards, ambitions, loyalties. Part of the ethical function of literature is the lesson of the value of diversity.

Of course, literature must operate within boundaries. (Like all human activities. The only boundless activity is being dead.) The problem is that the boundaries most people want to draw would choke off the freedom of literature to be what it can be, in all its inventiveness and capacity to be agitated.

We live in a culture committed to unifying greeds, and one of the world's vast and glorious multiplicity of languages, the one in which I speak and write, is now the dominant language. English has come to play, on a world scale and for vastly larger populations within the world's countries, a role similar to that played in medieval Europe by Latin.

But as we live in an increasingly global, transnational culture, we are also mired in increasingly fractionalized claims by real or newly self-constituted tribes. The old humanistic

ideas—of the republic of letters, of world literature—are under attack everywhere. They seem, to some, naïve, as well as
tainted by their origin in the great European ideal—some
would say Eurocentric ideal—of universal values.

The notions of "liberty" and of "rights" have under-
gone a striking degradation in recent years. In many communities, group rights are given greater weight than individual
rights.

In this respect, what makers of literature do *can*, implicitly, bolster the credibility of free expression, and of individual rights. Even when makers of literature have consecrated
their work to the service of the tribes or communities to
which they belong, their accomplishment as writers depends
on transcending this aim.

·

The qualities that make a given writer valuable or admirable can all be located within the singularity of the
writer's voice.

But this singularity, which is cultivated in private and is
the result of a long apprenticeship in reflection and in solitude, is constantly being tested by the social role writers feel
called on to play.

I do not question the *right* of the writer to engage in debate on public matters, to make common cause and practice
solidarity with like-minded others.

Nor is my point that such activity takes the writer far
from the reclusive, eccentric inner place where literature is
made. So do almost all the other activities that make up having a life.

But it's one thing to volunteer, stirred by the imperatives of conscience or of interest, to engage in public debate and public action. It's another to produce opinions—moralistic sound-bites—on demand.

Not: Been there, done that. But: For this, against that.

But a writer ought not to be an opinion-machine. As a black poet in my country put it, when reproached by some fellow African-Americans for not writing poems about the indignities of racism, "A writer is not a jukebox."

.

The writer's first job is not to have opinions but to tell the truth . . . and refuse to be an accomplice of lies and misinformation. Literature is the house of nuance and contrariness against the voices of simplification. The job of the writer is to make it harder to believe the mental despoilers. The job of the writer is to make us see the world as it is, full of many different claims and parts and experiences.

It is the job of the writer to depict the realities: the foul realities, the realities of rapture. It is the essence of the wisdom furnished by literature (the plurality of literary achievement) to help us to understand that, whatever is happening, something else is always going on.

I am haunted by that "something else."

I am haunted by the conflict of rights and of values I cherish. For instance that—sometimes—telling the truth does not further justice. That—sometimes—the furthering of justice may entail suppressing a good part of the truth.

Many of the twentieth century's most notable writers, in their activity as public voices, were accomplices in the suppression of truth to further what they understood to be (what *were*, in many cases) just causes.

My own view is, if I have to choose between truth and justice—of course, I don't want to choose—I choose truth.

．

Of course, I believe in righteous action. But is it the writer who acts?

These are three different things: *speaking*, what I am doing now; *writing*, what gives me whatever claim I have to this incomparable prize; and *being*, being a person who believes in active solidarity with others.

As Roland Barthes once observed: "Who *speaks* is not who *writes*, and who *writes* is not who *is*."

And of course I have opinions, political opinions, some of them formed on the basis of reading and discussing, and reflecting, but not from first-hand experience. Let me share with you two opinions of mine—quite predictable opinions, in the light of public positions I've taken on matters about which I have some direct knowledge.

I believe that the doctrine of collective responsibility, as a rationale for collective punishment, is never justified, militarily or ethically. I mean the use of disproportionate firepower against civilians, the demolition of their homes and destruction of their orchards and groves, the deprivation of their livelihood and their right to employment, schooling, medical services, untrammeled access to neighboring towns and communities . . . all as a punishment for hostile military activity that may or may not even be in the vicinity of these civilians.

I also believe that there can be no peace here until the planting of Israeli communities in the Territories is halted

and is followed—sooner rather than later—by the disman-
tling of these settlements and the withdrawal of the military
units amassed there to guard them.

I wager that these two opinions of mine are shared by
many people here in this hall. I suspect that—to use an old
American expression—I'm preaching to the choir.

But do I hold these opinions as a writer? Or do I not hold
them as a person of conscience and then use my position as a
writer to add my voice to others saying the same thing? The
influence a writer can exert is purely adventitious. It is, now,
an aspect of the culture of celebrity.

There is something vulgar about public dissemination of
opinions on matters about which one does not have extensive
first-hand knowledge. If I speak of what I do not know, or
know hastily, this is mere opinion-mongering.

I say this, to return to the beginning, as a matter of
honor. The honor of literature. The project of having an individual voice. Serious writers, creators of literature, shouldn't
just express themselves differently from the hegemonic discourse of the mass media. They should be in opposition to the
communal drone of the newscast and the talk show.

The problem with opinions is that one is stuck with
them. And whenever writers are functioning as writers, they
always see . . . more.

Whatever there is, there is always more. Whatever is
happening, something else is going on, too.

If literature itself, this great enterprise that has been conducted (within our purview) for nearly three millennia, embodies a wisdom—and I think it does and is at the heart of the
importance we give to literature—it is by demonstrating the
multiple nature of our private and our communal destinies. It

will remind us that there can be contradictions, sometimes irreducible conflicts, among the values we most cherish. (This is what is meant by "tragedy.") It will remind us of the "also" and "the something else."

The wisdom of literature is quite antithetical to having opinions. "Nothing is my last word about anything," said Henry James. Furnishing opinions, even correct opinions—whenever asked—cheapens what novelists and poets do best, which is to sponsor reflectiveness, to pursue complexity.

Information will never replace illumination. But something that sounds like, except that it's better than, information—I mean the condition of being *informed*; I mean concrete, specific, detailed, historically dense, first-hand knowledge—is the indispensable prerequisite for a writer to express opinions in public.

Let the others, the celebrities and the politicians, talk down to us; lie. If being both a writer and a public voice could stand for anything better, it would be that writers would consider the formulation of opinions and judgments to be a difficult responsibility.

Another problem with opinions. They are agencies of self-immobilization. What writers do should free us up, shake us up. Open avenues of compassion and new interests. Remind us that we might, just might, aspire to become different, and better, than we are. Remind us that we can change.

As Cardinal Newman said, "In a higher world it is otherwise, but here below to live is to change, and to be perfect is to have changed often."

And what do I mean by the word "perfection"? That I shall not try to explain but only say, Perfection makes me laugh. Not cynically, I hasten to add. With joy.

•

I am grateful to have been awarded the Jerusalem Prize. I accept it as an honor to all those committed to the enterprise of literature. I accept it in homage to all the writers and readers in Israel and in Palestine struggling to create literature made of singular voices and the multiplicity of truths. I accept the prize in the name of peace and the reconciliation of injured and fearful communities. Necessary peace. Necessary concessions and new arrangements. Necessary abatement of stereotypes. Necessary persistence of dialogue. I accept the prize—this international prize, sponsored by an international book fair—as an event that honors, above all, the international republic of letters.

The World as India

The St. Jerome Lecture on Literary Translation

•

IN MEMORIAM W. G. SEBALD

To translate means many things, among them: to circulate, to transport, to disseminate, to explain, to make (more) accessible. I'll start with the proposition—the exaggeration, if you will—that by literary translation we mean, we could mean, the translation of the small percentage of published books actually worth reading: that is to say, worth *re*reading. I shall argue that a proper consideration of the art of literary translation is essentially a claim for the value of literature itself. Beyond the obvious need for the translator's facilitations in creating stock for literature as a small, prestigious import-export business, beyond the indispensable role that translation has in the construction of literature as a competitive sport, played both nationally and internationally (with rivalries, teams, and lucrative prizes)—beyond the mercantile and the agonistic and the ludic incentives for doing translation lies an older, frankly evangelical incentive, more difficult to avow in these self-consciously impious times.

In what I call the evangelical incentive, the purpose of translation is to enlarge the readership of a book deemed to be important. It assumes that some books are discernibly better than other books, that literary merit exists in a pyramidal shape, and it is imperative for the works near the top to become available to as many as possible, which means to be widely translated and as frequently retranslated as is feasible. Clearly, such a view of literature assumes that a rough consensus can be reached on which works are essential. It does *not* entail thinking the consensus—or canon—is fixed for all time and cannot be modified.

At the top of the pyramid are the books regarded as scripture: indispensable or essential exoteric knowledge that, by definition, invites translation. (Probably the most linguistically influential translations have been translations of the Bible: Saint Jerome, Luther, Tyndale, the Authorized Version.) Translation is then first of all making better known what deserves to be better known—because it is improving, deepening, exalting; because it is an indispensable legacy from the past; because it is a contribution to knowledge, sacred or other. In a more secular register, translation was also thought to bring a benefit to the translator: translating was a valuable cognitive—and ethical—workout.

In the era when it is proposed that computers— "translating machines"—will soon be able to perform most translating tasks, what we call literary translation perpetuates the traditional sense of what translation entails. The new view is that translation is the finding of equivalents; or to vary the metaphor, that a translation is a problem, for which solutions can be devised. In contrast, the old understanding is that translation is the making of choices, conscious choices, choices not simply between the stark dichotomies of good and bad, correct and incorrect, but among a more complex dispersion of alternatives, such as "good" versus "better" and "better" versus "best," not to mention such impure alternatives as "old-fashioned" versus "trendy," "vulgar" versus "pretentious," and "abbreviated" versus "wordy."

For such choices to be good—or better—was assumed to imply knowledge, both wide and deep, on the part of the translator. Translating, which is here seen as an activity of choosing in the larger sense, was a profession of individuals who were the bearers of a certain inward culture. To translate thoughtfully, painstakingly, ingeniously, respectfully was a precise measure of the translator's fealty to the enterprise of literature itself.

Choices that might be thought of as merely linguistic always imply ethical standards as well, which has made the activity of translating itself the vehicle of such values as integrity, responsibility, fidelity, boldness, humility. The ethical understanding of the task of the translator originated in the awareness that translation is basically an impossible task, if what is meant is that the translator is able to take up the text of an author written in one language and deliver it, intact, without loss, into another language. Obviously, this is *not* what is being stressed by those who await impatiently the supersession of the dilemmas of the translator by the equivalencings of better, more ingenious translating machines.

Literary translation is a branch of literature—anything but a mechanical task. But what makes translation so complex an undertaking is that it responds to a variety of aims. There are demands that arise from the nature of literature as a form of communication. There is the mandate, with a work regarded as essential, to make it known to the widest possible audience. There is the general difficulty of passing from one language to another, and the special intransigence of certain texts, which points to something inherent in the work quite outside the intentions or awareness of its author that emerges as the cycle of translations begins—a quality that, for want of a better word, we call translatability.

This nest of complex questions is often reduced to the perennial debate among translators—the debate about literalness—that dates back at least to ancient Rome, when Greek literature was translated into Latin, and continues to exercise translators in every country (and with respect to which there is a variety of national traditions and biases). The oldest theme of the discussion of translations is the role of accuracy and fidelity. Surely there must have been translators in the ancient world whose standard was strict literal fidelity (and damn euphony!), a position defended with dazzling obstinacy by Vladimir Nabokov in his Englishing of *Eugene Onegin*. How else to explain the bold insistence of Saint Jerome himself (ca. 331–420)—the intellectual in the ancient world who (adapting arguments first broached by Cicero) reflected most extensively, in prefaces and in letters, on the task of translation—that the inevitable result of aiming at a faithful reproduction of the author's words and images is the sacrifice of meaning and of grace?

This passage is from the preface Jerome wrote to his translation into Latin of the *Chronicle* of Eusebius. (He translated it in the years A.D. 381–82, while he was living in Constantinople in order to take part in the Council—six years before he settled in Bethlehem, to improve his knowledge of Hebrew, and almost a decade before he began the epochal task of translating the Hebrew Bible into Latin.) Of this early translation from Greek, Jerome wrote:

> It has long been the practice of learned men to exercise their minds by rendering into Latin the works of Greek writers, and, what is more difficult, to translate the poems of illustrious authors though trammelled by the farther requirements of verse. It was thus that our Tully literally translated whole books of Plato . . . [and later] amused himself with the economics of Xenophon. In this latter work the golden river of eloquence again and again meets with obstacles, around which its waters break and foam to such an extent that persons unacquainted with the original would not believe they were reading Cicero's words. And no wonder! It is hard to follow another man's lines . . . It is an arduous task to preserve felicity and grace unimpaired in a translation. Some word has forcibly expressed a given thought; I have no word of my own to convey the meaning; and while I am seeking to satisfy the sense I may go a long way round and accomplish but a small distance of my journey. Then we must take into account the ins and outs of transposition, the variations in cases, the diversity of figures, and, lastly, the peculiar, and, so to speak, the native idiom of the language. A literal translation sounds absurd; if, on the other hand, I am obliged to change either the order or the words themselves, I shall appear to have forsaken the duty of a translator. (tr. W. H. Fremantle, 1892)

What is striking about this self-justifying passage is Jerome's concern that his readers understand just how daunting a task literary translation is. What we read in translation, he declares later in the same preface, is necessarily an impoverishment of the original.

> If any one thinks that the grace of language does not suffer through translation, let him render Homer word for word into Latin. I will go farther and say that, if he will translate this author into the prose of his own language, the order of the words will seem ridiculous, and the most eloquent of poets almost dumb.

What is the best way to deal with this inherent impossibility of translation? For Jerome there can be no doubt how to proceed, as he explains over and over in the prefaces he wrote to his various translations. In a letter to Pammachius, written in A.D. 396, he quotes Cicero to affirm that the only proper way to translate is

> . . . keeping the sense but altering the form by adapting both the metaphors and the words to suit our own language. I have not deemed it necessary to render word for word but I have reproduced the general style and emphasis.

Later in the same letter, quoting Evagrius this time—one must assume that there were many critics and cavillers—he declares defiantly: "A literal translation from one language into another obscures the sense." If this makes the translator a coauthor of the book, so be it. "The truth is," Jerome writes in his preface to Eusebius, "that I have partly discharged the office of a translator and partly that of a writer."

The matter could hardly be put with greater boldness or relevance to contemporary reflections. How far is the translator empowered to adapt—that is, *re-create*—the text in the language into which the work is being translated? If word-by-word fidelity and literary excellence in the new language are incompatible, how "free" can a responsible translation be? Is it the first task of the translator to efface the foreignness of a text, and to recast it according to the norms of the new language? There is no serious translator who does not fret about such problems: like classical ballet, literary translation is an activity with unrealistic standards, that is, standards so exacting that they are bound to generate dissatisfaction, a sense of being rarely up to the mark, among ambitious practitioners. And like classical ballet, literary translation is an art of repertory. Works deemed major are regularly redone—because the adaptation now seems too free, not accurate enough; or the translation is thought to contain too many errors; or the idiom, which seemed transparent to the contemporaries of a translation, now seems dated.

Dancers are trained to strive for the not entirely chimerical goal of perfection: exemplary, error-free expressiveness. In a literary translation, given the multiple imperatives to which a literary translation has to respond, there can only be a superior, never a perfect, performance. Translation, by definition, always entails some loss of the original substance. All translations are sooner or later revealed as imperfect and eventually, even in the case of the most exemplary performances, come to be regarded as provisional.

•

Saint Jerome was doing translations—from Hebrew and from Greek—into Latin. The language into which he was translating was, and was to remain for many centuries, an international language.

I am giving this talk in the new international language, estimated to be the mother tongue of more than 350 million people, and spoken as a second language by tens of millions of people throughout the world.

I am here in England, where the language I am speaking and in which I write was born. I shall take the simple view that we are *not* divided by a common language, as the old quip has it. And in my country, we don't call the language most of us speak "American" (for all that the title page of the French translations of my books say *"traduit de l'américain"*). Apparently, however, there are people in the United States who don't know why they call it English.

Some years ago an English friend of mine, a writer with a rich Oxbridge accent, visited America for the first time with his wife and teenage daughters and decided the best way to have the whole American experience was to rent a car and drive across the country, from New York to California. Stopping at a filling station somewhere in Iowa on a sweltering summer day, my friend was asked by the lone attendant servicing his car, following a few moments of chat, "Where do you folks come from?" "England," replied my friend, wondering what *that* might provoke. "No kidding," exclaimed the filling station attendant. "You really speak English very well for a foreigner."

Of course, most of us do know why it's called English. And it is the glory of the literature of my country, which is not much more than two hundred years old, that it gets to be written in your thousand-year-old language.

Each day I sit down to write, I marvel at the richness of the language I am privileged to use. But my pride in English is somewhat at odds with my awareness of another kind of linguistic privilege: to write in a language that everyone, in principle, is obliged to—desires to—understand.

Though seemingly identical now with the world dominance of the colossal and unique superpower of which I am a citizen, the initial ascendancy to international lingua franca of the tongue in which Shakespeare wrote was something of a fluke. One of the key moments was the adoption in the 1920s (I believe) of English as the international language of civilian aviation. For planes to circulate with safety, those who flew them and those who directed their flight had to have a language in common. An Italian pilot landing in Vienna speaks to the tower in English. An Austrian pilot landing in Naples speaks to the tower in English. More, it produces the oddity that an Italian plane going from Naples to Palermo, a Swedish pilot going from Stockholm to Malmö, a Brazilian pilot going from São Paulo to Rio—each should be communicating with the tower in English. We take this for granted now.

More powerfully, and I think decisively, the ubiquity of computers—the vehicle of another form of transport: *mental transport*—has required a dominant language. While the instructions on your interface are likely to be in your native language, going online and using search engines—that is, circulating internationally on the computer—requires a knowledge of English.

English has become the common language that unifies linguistic disparities. India has sixteen "official languages" (actually, many more vernacular languages are spoken), and there is no way that India, given its present composition and diversity, which includes 180 million Muslims, is ever going to agree to, say, the principal language, Hindi, becoming the national language. The language that could be a national language would precisely not be a native one but the language of the conqueror, of the colonial era. Just because it is alien, foreign, it can become the unifying language of a permanently diverse people: the only language that all Indians might have in common not only is, it has to be, English.

The computer has only reinforced the preeminence of English in our global India. Surely the most interesting linguistic phenomena of our era are, on the one hand, the disappearance of many lesser languages—that is, languages spoken by very small, isolated, impoverished peoples—and the unique success of English, which now has a status unlike any other language used on the planet. English is now advancing in every part of the world, through the dominance of English-speaking media—which means media in which English is spoken with an American accent—and the need for business people and scientists to communicate in a common tongue.

We live in a world that is, in several important respects, both mired in the most banal nationalisms and radically post-national. The primary feature of the trade barriers may fall, money may become multinational (like the dollar, which is the currency in several Latin American countries, and of course the euro). But there is one intractable feature of our lives that roots us in the old boundaries that advanced capitalism, advanced science and technology, and advanced imperial dominance (American style) find so encumbering. That is the fact that we speak so many different languages.

Hence the necessity of an international language. And what more plausible candidate than English?

This globalization of English has had an already-perceptible effect on the fortunes of literature, that is, of translation. I suspect that fewer literary works of foreign literature, especially from the languages felt to be less important, are being translated into English than, say, twenty or thirty years ago. But many more books written in English are being translated into foreign languages. It is now extremely rare for foreign novels to appear on the *New York Times* bestseller list, as they did twenty, thirty, fifty years ago. Celebrated novels by Kundera and García Márquez and Lampedusa and Pasternak and Grass were bestsellers in the United States. A little over a half-century ago Thomas Mann's *Doctor Faustus* was for a time number one on the bestseller list—inconceivable today.

.

It is often taken for granted that the aim of a translation is to make the work "sound" as if it were written in the language into which it is being translated.

Translation being an activity not only practiced in every nation but subject to national traditions, there are greater pressures in some countries than in others to efface as much as possible the evidence of foreignness. France has a particularly strong tradition of translation as adaptation, at the expense of strict fidelity to the text. I have often been told by my French publishers, when I pointed out flagrant inaccuracies in a translation of one of my books: "Yes, true . . . but it reads very well in French." When I hear that my book or someone else's, thanks to the translator's efforts, now reads very well in French, I know that the book has been reshaped according to existing conventions (usually not the most fastidious ones) of contemporary French prose. But since my prose in English is not always conventional in its rhythms or its lexical choices, I can be sure that this is *not* being transmitted into French. Only the sense—and only a part of that (because the sense seems to me connected essentially with whatever is odd about my prose)—is being transmitted.

The first, and still perhaps definitive, criticism of the idea—so powerfully expounded by Jerome—that it is the job of the translator to completely recast the work to suit the spirit of the new language was made by the German Protestant theologian Friedrich Schleiermacher (1768–1834) in his great essay "On the Different Methods of Translation," written in 1813.

In arguing that "reading well" is not the primary standard of merit in translation, Schleiermacher does not, of course, mean all translations but only literary translations—those that involve what he calls, appealingly, "the sacred seriousness of language." As for the rest, he writes:

> . . . as nations appear to mix in our time to a greater extent than they did before, the marketplace is everywhere and these are conversations of the marketplace, whether they are social or literary or political, and really do not belong in the translator's domain but rather in that of the interpreter. (tr. André Lefevere)

For Schleiermacher, translation—which is far more than a service to commerce, to the marketplace—is a complex necessity. There is the intrinsic value of making known, across a linguistic border, an essential text. There is also a value in connecting with something that is different from what we know, with foreignness itself.

For Schleiermacher, a literary text is not just its sense. It is, first of all, the language in which it is written. And as each person has a core identity, each person has, essentially, only one language.

> Just as a man must decide to belong to one country, he must adhere to one language, or he will float without any bearings above an unpleasant middle ground. It is right that even now Latin is being written among us as the language of officialdom, to keep alive the consciousness that this was the scholarly and sacred mother tongue of our ancestors; it is good that this should also happen in the field of the common European economy, to make commerce easier; but in that case, too, it will succeed only to the extent that the object is everything for such a representation and that one's own opinion and the way in which one combines objects counts for very little.

Substitute English for Latin in Schleiermacher's extremely reserved encomium for a pan-European (read: global) language required to facilitate pan-European (read: global) technical and scientific exchanges, and you will see how little he expects of this language as a medium of subjective, that is, literary expression.

In the matter of concrete practice, Schleiermacher takes up the exact opposite of Jerome's position, arguing that the translator's primary duty is to stay as close as possible to the original text, with the understanding that the result will, precisely, read as a translation. To naturalize a foreign book is to lose what is most valuable about it: the spirit of the language, the mental ethos out of which the text emerges. Therefore if a translation from, say, French or Russian into German sounds as if it were originally written in German, the German-speaking reader will be deprived of the knowledge of otherness that comes from reading something that actually does sound foreign.

The difference between Jerome's and Schleiermacher's position is the difference made by the interposition of the idea of national identity as the framework around which linguistic separateness coheres. For Jerome, to speak another language was not to be another kind of person. Jerome lived in a world that was, in ways not unlike our own, significantly transnational or international. For Schleiermacher, to speak another language was to become, in the deepest sense, inauthentic. He writes:

> . . . the aim of translating in a way such as the author would have originally written in the language of the translation is not only out of reach, but also null and void in itself, for whoever acknowledges the shaping power of language, as it is one with the peculiar character of a nation, must concede that every most excellent human being has acquired his knowledge, as well as the possibility of expressing it, in and through language, and that no one therefore adheres to his language mechanically as if he were strapped into it . . . and that no one could change languages in his thinking as he

pleases the way one can easily change a span of horses and replace it with another; rather everyone produces original work in his mother tongue only, so that the question cannot even be raised of how he would have written his works in another language.

Schleiermacher is not, of course, denying that there is such a thing as the ability to speak and to write in more than one language. But he is assuming that everyone has a "mother tongue," and the relation to other languages in which one might speak, or even write poetry and philosophize, would somehow be not "organic"—a favorite metaphor of the period. This is, clearly, an ideological position: many peoples have been duoglot, if not polyglot. Italy, for example, where one might speak not only Tuscan (so-called Italian) but also Neapolitan or Romagnolo. Québec, where educated people speak both French and English. In the old Austro-Hungarian Empire, most educated people in the countries now called Austria, the Czech Republic, Romania, and Hungary spoke at least two, sometimes three languages every day. Clearly, Schleiermacher's position is not merely a descriptive one. (His deep agenda has to do with his notion of nationhood and peoplehood.) In Schleiermacher's view, it is not that one cannot, but that one *should* not deploy two languages as equals. The epitome of inauthenticity would be to assume that one could inhabit another language in the same spirit that one could one's own.

·

But can one authentically speak more than one language? Schleiermacher's question continues to reverberate. What does mastery of a second language mean?

I have been told by American and English friends who are longtime residents of Japan (most with Japanese spouses) that the Japanese typically regard with great suspicion, and even a touch of hostility, a foreigner who speaks their language without making mistakes. But probably this prejudice will fade, as Japan continues to accept that the existence of foreigners in its midst is not an oddity or a misfortune or an adulteration of the national essence.

At the other extreme, a more recent example of what is involved in attaining perfect mastery in a second language—which happens to be English—give us a perfect Schleiermachian scenario of inauthenticity. I am thinking about one flourishing enterprise in the multibillion-dollar software industry now so important to the Indian economy. These are the call centers, employing many thousands of young women and men who give technical help or take reservations made by dialing 1-800 (that is, toll-free numbers all over the United States). The young people, all of whom already speak English, who compete successfully for these coveted jobs in the call centers, and have completed the arduous course designed to erase all traces of their Indian accent in English (many fail), are being paid what is a munificent salary for office work in India, though of course far less than what IBM, American Express, GE, Delta Airlines, and chains of hotels and restaurants would have to pay to Americans to do the job—reason enough for more and more such tasks to be "outsourced." It also seems to be the case that the Indians perform the tasks better, with fewer errors, which is not surprising, since virtually all of them have college degrees.

From large floors of office buildings in Bangalore or Bombay or New Delhi, call after call is answered by young

Indians seated in rows of small booths ("Hi, this is Nancy. How may I help you?"), each equipped with a computer that allows them to summon with a few clicks the relevant information to make a reservation, maps to give information about the best highway route, weather forecasts, and so forth.

Nancy, or Mary Lou, Betty, Sally Jane, Megan, Bill, Jim, Wally, Frank—these cheerful voices had first to be trained for months, by instructors and by tapes, to acquire a pleasant middle-American (not an educated American) accent, and to learn basic American slang, informal idioms (including regional ones), and elementary mass-culture references (TV personalities and the plots and protagonists of the main sitcoms, the latest blockbuster in the multiplex, fresh baseball and basketball scores, and such), so that if the exchange with the client in the United States becomes prolonged, they will not falter with the small talk and will have the means to continue to pass for Americans.

To pull this off, they have to be plausibly American to themselves. They have been assigned American names and little biographies of their American identities: place and date of birth, parents' occupation, number of siblings, religious denomination (almost always Protestant), high school, favorite sport, favorite kind of music, marital status, and the like. If asked where they are, they have a reply. For example, if the client is calling from Savannah, Georgia, to make a reservation in a hotel in Macon, Georgia, and is asking directions for the quickest way to drive from Savannah to Macon, the operator might say she or he is in Atlanta. Letting on that they are in Bangalore, India, would get pretend-Nancy or pretend-Bill instantly fired. (All the calls are routinely, and undetectably, monitored by supervisors.) And of course virtually none of these young people has ever left home.

Would "Nancy" and "Bill" prefer to be a real Nancy and a real Bill? Almost all say—there have been interviews—that they would. Would they want to come to America, where it would be normal to speak English all the time with an American accent? Of course they would.

.

Our ideas about literature (and therefore about translation) are necessarily reactive. In the early nineteenth century it seemed progressive to champion national literatures, and the distinctiveness (the special "genius") of the national languages. The prestige of the nation-state in the nineteenth century was fueled by the consciousness of having produced great "national" writers—in countries such as Poland and Hungary, these were usually poets. Indeed, the national idea had a particularly libertarian inflection in the smaller European countries, still existing within the confines of an imperial system, which were moving toward the identity of nation-states.

Concern for the authenticity of the linguistic embodiment of literature was one response to these new ideas and gave rise to intense support for writing in dialects or in so-called regional languages. Another altogether different response to the idea of national identity was that of Goethe, who was perhaps the first to broach—and at a time, the early nineteenth century, when the idea of national identity was most progressive—the project of world literature (*Weltliteratur*).

It may seem surprising that Goethe could have fielded a notion so far ahead of its time. It seems less odd if one thinks of Goethe as not only Napoleon's contemporary but as Napoleonic himself in more than a few projects and ideas that could be the intellectual equivalent of the Napoleonic imperium. His idea of world literature recalls Napoleon's idea of a United States of Europe, since by "the world" Goethe meant Europe and the neo-European countries, where there was already much literary traffic over borders. In Goethe's perspective, the dignity and specificity of national languages (intimately tied to the affirmations of nationalism) are entirely compatible with the idea of a world literature, which is a notion of a world readership: reading books in translation.

Later in the nineteenth century internationalism or cosmopolitanism in literature became, in powerful countries, the more progressive notion, the one with the libertarian inflection. Progress would be the natural development of literature from "provincial" to "national" to "international." A notion of *Weltliteratur* flourished through most of the twentieth century, with its recurrent dream of an international parliament in which all nation-states would sit as equals. Literature would be such an international system, which creates an even greater role for translations, so we could all be reading each other's books. The global spread of English could even be regarded as an essential move toward transforming literature into a truly worldwide system of production and exchange.

But, as many have observed, globalization is a process that brings quite uneven benefits to the various peoples that make up the human population, and the globalization of English has not altered the history of prejudices about national identities, one result of which is that some languages—and the literature produced in them—have always been considered more important than others. An example. Surely Machado de Assis's *The*

Posthumous Memories of Brás Cubas and *Dom Casmurro* and Aluísio Azevedo's *The Slum*, three of the best novels written anywhere in the last part of the nineteenth century, would be as famous as a late-nineteenth-century literary masterpiece *can* be now had they been written not in Portuguese by Brazilians but in German or French or Russian. Or English. (It is not a question of big versus small languages. Brazil hardly lacks for inhabitants, and Portuguese is the sixth most widely spoken language in the world.) I hasten to add that these wonderful books *are* translated, excellently, into English. The problem is that they don't get mentioned. It has not—at least not yet—been deemed necessary for someone cultivated, someone looking for the ecstasy that only fiction can bring, to read them.

The ancient biblical image suggests that we live in our differences, emblematically linguistic, on top of one another—like Frank Lloyd Wright's dream of a mile-high apartment building. But common sense tells us our linguistic dispersion cannot be a tower. The geography of our dispersal into many languages is much more horizontal than vertical (or so it seems), with rivers and mountains and valleys, and oceans that lap around the land mass. To translate is to ferry, to bring across.

But maybe there is some truth in the image. A tower has many levels, and the many tenants of this tower are stacked one on top of the other. If Babel is anything like other towers, the higher floors are the more coveted. Maybe certain languages occupy whole sections of the upper floors, the great rooms and commanding terraces. And other languages and their literary products are confined to lower floors, low ceilings, blocked views.

·

Some sixteen centuries after Saint Jerome, but barely more than a century after Schleiermacher's landmark essay on translation, came the third of what are for me the exemplary reflections on the project and duties of the translator. It is the essay entitled "The Task of the Translator" that Walter Benjamin wrote in 1923 as a preface to his translation of Baudelaire's *Tableaux parisiens*.

In bringing Baudelaire's French into German, he tells us, he is not obliged to make Baudelaire sound as if he had written in German. On the contrary, his obligation is to maintain the sense that the German reader might have of something different. He writes:

> All translation is only a somewhat provisional way of coming to terms with the foreignness of languages . . . It is not the highest praise of a translation, particularly in the age of its origin, to say that it reads as if it had originally been written in that language. (tr. Harry Zohn)

The opportunity offered by translation is not a defensive one: to preserve, to embalm, the current state of the translator's own language. Rather, he argues, it is an opportunity to allow a foreign tongue to influence and modify the language into which a work is being translated. Benjamin's reason for preferring a translation that reveals its foreignness is quite different from Schleiermacher's. It is not because he wishes to promote the autonomy and integrity of individual languages. Benjamin's thinking is at the opposite pole to any nationalist agenda. It is a metaphysical consideration, arising from his idea of the very nature of language, according to which language itself demands the translator's exertions.

Every language is part of language, which is larger than any single language. Every individual literary work is a part of literature, which is larger than the literature of any single language.

It is something like this view—which would place translation at the center of the literary enterprise—that I have tried to support with these remarks.

It is the nature of literature as we now understand it—understand it rightly, I believe—to circulate, for diverse and necessarily impure motives. Translation is the circulatory system of the world's literatures. Literary translation, I think, is preeminently an ethical task, and one that mirrors and duplicates the role of literature itself, which is to extend our sympathies; to educate the heart and mind; to create inwardness; to secure and deepen the awareness (with all its consequences) that other people, people different from us, really do exist.

·

I am old enough to have grown up, in the American Southwest, thinking there was something called literature in English, of which American literature was a branch. The writer who mattered most to me as a child was Shakespeare—Shakespeare as a reading experience (actually, a reading-aloud experience), which started with my being given a prettily illustrated edition of Charles Lamb's *Tales of Shakespeare* when I was eight; my reading of Lamb and then of many of the plays predated by four years my actually seeing Shakespeare on the stage or in a film adaptation. And besides Shakespeare, retold or straight, there was Winnie-the-Pooh and *The Secret Garden* and *Gulliver's Travels* and the Brontës (first *Jane Eyre*, then *Wuthering Heights*) and *The Cloister and the Hearth* and Dick-

ens (the first were *David Copperfield* and *A Christmas Carol*
and *A Tale of Two Cities*) and lots of Stevenson (*Kidnapped,
Treasure Island, Dr. Jekyll and Mr. Hyde*), and Oscar Wilde's
The Happy Prince . . . Of course, there were American books,
too, like the tales of Poe and *Little Women* and novels of Jack
London and *Ramona*. But in that distant, still reflexively gen-
teel, culturally Anglophile era, it seemed perfectly normal that
most of the books I read should come from somewhere else,
somewhere older, such as faraway, thrillingly exotic England.

When the "somewhere else" grew larger, when my
reading—always in English, of course—came to include
wonderful books that had not originally been written in English, when I moved on to world literature, the transition was
almost imperceptible. Dumas, Hugo, and on from there . . .
I knew I was now reading "foreign" writers. It didn't occur to
me to ponder over the mediation that brought these ever-
more-awesome books to me. (Question: Who is the greatest
Russian writer of the nineteenth century? Answer: Constance
Garnett.) Had I recognized an awkward sentence in a novel
I was reading by Mann or Balzac or Tolstoy, it would not have
occurred to me to wonder if the sentence read as awkwardly
in the original German or French or Russian, or to suspect
that the sentence might have been "badly" translated. To my
young, beginning reader's mind, there was no such thing as
a bad translation. There were only translations—which de-
coded books to which I would otherwise not have had access,
and put them into my hands and heart. As far as I was concerned, the original text and the translation were as one.

The very first time I raised to myself the problem of a poor
translation was when I started going to the opera, in Chicago,
when I was sixteen. There I held in my hands for the first time

an *en face* translation—the original language on the left (by this time I had some French and Italian) and the English on the right—and I was stunned and mystified by the blatant inaccuracy of the translations. (It was to be many years before I understood why the words in a libretto cannot be translated literally.) Opera excepted, I never asked myself, in those early years of reading literature in translation, about what I was missing. It was as if I felt it were my job, as a passionate reader, to see *through* the faults or limitations of a translation—as one sees through (or looks past) the scratches on a bad print of a beloved old film one is seeing once again. Translations were a gift, for which I would always be grateful. What—rather, who—would I be without Dostoyevsky and Tolstoy and Chekhov?

My sense of what literature can be, my reverence for the practice of literature as a vocation, and my identification of the vocation of the writer with the exercise of freedom—all these constituent elements of my sensibility are inconceivable without the books I read in translation from an early age. Literature was mental travel: travel into the past . . . and to other countries. (Literature was the vehicle that could take you *anywhere*.) And literature was criticism of one's own reality, in the light of a better standard.

A writer is first of all a reader. It is from reading that I derive the standards by which I measure my own work and according to which I fall lamentably short. It is from reading, even before writing, that I became part of a community—the community of literature—which includes more dead than living writers. Reading, and having standards, are then relations with the past and with what is other. Reading and having standards for literature are, indispensably in my view, relations with literature in translation.

On Courage and Resistance

The Oscar Romero Award Keynote Address

Allow me to invoke not one but two, only two, who were heroes—among millions of heroes. Who were victims—among tens of millions of victims.

The first: Oscar Arnulfo Romero, Archbishop of San Salvador, murdered in his vestments, while saying mass in the cathedral on March 24, 1980—twenty-three years ago—because he had become "a vocal advocate of a just peace, and had openly opposed the forces of violence and oppression." (I am quoting from the description of the Oscar Romero Award, being given today to Ishai Menuchin.)

The second: Rachel Corrie, a twenty-three-year-old college student from Olympia, Washington, murdered in the bright neon-orange jacket with Day-Glo striping that "human shields" wear to make themselves quite visible, and possibly safer, while trying to stop one of the almost daily house demolitions by Israeli forces in Rafah, a town in the southern

Gaza Strip (where Gaza abuts the Egyptian border), on March 16, 2003—two weeks ago. Standing in front of a Palestinian physician's house that had been targeted for demolition, Corrie, one of eight young American and British human-shield volunteers in Rafah, had been waving and shouting at the driver of an oncoming armored D-9 bulldozer through her megaphone, then dropped to her knees in the path of the supersized bulldozer . . . which did not slow down.

Two emblematic figures of sacrifice, killed by the forces of violence and oppression to which they were offering non-violent, principled, dangerous opposition.

.

Let's start with risk. The risk of being punished. The risk of being isolated. The risk of being injured or killed. The risk of being scorned.

We are all conscripts in one sense or another. For all of us, it is hard to break ranks; to incur the disapproval, the censure, the violence of an offended majority with a different idea of loyalty. We shelter under banner words like justice, peace, and reconciliation that enroll us in new, if much smaller and relatively powerless, communities of the like-minded. That mobilize us for the demonstration, the protest, and the public performance of acts of civil disobedience—not for the parade ground and the battlefield.

To fall out of step with one's tribe; to step beyond one's tribe into a world that is larger mentally but smaller numerically—if alienation or dissidence is not your habitual or gratifying posture, this is a complex, difficult process.

It is hard to defy the wisdom of the tribe: the wisdom that values the lives of members of the tribe above all others.

It will always be unpopular—it will always be deemed un-patriotic—to say that the lives of the members of the other tribe are as valuable as one's own.

It is easier to give one's allegiance to those we know, to those we see, to those with whom we are embedded, to those with whom we share—as we may—a community of fear.

Let's not underestimate the force of what we oppose. Let's not underestimate the retaliation that may be visited on those who dare to dissent from the brutalities and repressions thought justified by the fears of the majority.

We are flesh. We can be punctured by a bayonet, torn apart by a suicide bomber. We can be crushed by a bulldozer, gunned down in a cathedral.

Fear binds people together. And fear disperses them. Courage inspires communities: the courage of an example—for courage is as contagious as fear. But courage, certain kinds of courage, can also isolate the brave.

The perennial destiny of principles: while everyone professes to have them, they are likely to be sacrificed when they become inconveniencing. Generally a moral principle is something that puts one at *variance* with accepted practice. And that variance has consequences, sometimes unpleasant consequences, as the community takes its revenge on those who challenge its contradictions—who want a society actually to uphold the principles it professes to defend.

The standard that a society should actually embody its own professed principles is a utopian one, in the sense that moral principles contradict the way things really are—and always will be. How things really are—and always will be—is neither all evil nor all good but deficient, inconsistent, inferior. Principles invite us to do something about the morass of contradictions in which we function morally. Principles invite us to clean up our act, to become intolerant of moral laxity and compromise and cowardice and the turning away from what is upsetting: that secret gnawing of the heart that tells us that what we are doing is *not* right, and so counsels us that we'd be better off just *not* thinking about it.

The cry of the antiprincipled: "I'm doing the best I can." The best given the circumstances, of course.

•

Let's say the principle is: it's wrong to oppress and humiliate a whole people. To deprive them systematically of lodging and proper nutrition; to destroy their habitations, means of livelihood, access to education and medical care, and ability to consort with one another.

That these practices are wrong, whatever the provocation.

And there is provocation. That, too, should not be denied.

•

At the center of our moral life and our moral imagination are the great models of resistance: the great stories of those who have said no. No, I will not serve.

What models, what stories? A Mormon may resist the outlawing of polygamy. An antiabortion militant may resist the law that has made abortion legal. They, too, will invoke the claims of religion (or faith) and morality against the edicts of civil society. Appeal to the existence of a higher law that authorizes us to defy the laws of the state can be used to justify criminal transgression as well as the noblest struggle for justice.

Courage has no moral value in itself, for courage is not, in itself, a moral virtue. Vicious scoundrels, murderers, terrorists may be brave. To describe courage as a virtue, we need an adjective: we speak of "moral courage"—because there is such a thing as amoral courage, too.

And resistance has no value in itself. It is the *content* of the resistance that determines its merit, its moral necessity.

Let's say: resistance to a criminal war. Let's say: resistance to the occupation and annexation of another people's land.

Again: there is nothing inherently superior about resistance. All our claims for the righteousness of resistance rest on the rightness of the claim that the resisters are acting in the name of justice. And the justice of the cause does not depend on, and is not enhanced by, the virtue of those who make the assertion. It depends first and last on the truth of a description of a state of affairs that is, truly, unjust and unnecessary.

.

Here is what I believe to be a truthful description of a state of affairs that has taken me many years of uncertainty, ignorance, and anguish to acknowledge.

A wounded and fearful country, Israel, is going through the greatest crisis of its turbulent history, brought about by the policy of steadily increasing and reinforcing settlements on the territories won after its victory in the Arab-Israeli war of 1967. The decision of successive Israeli governments to retain control over the West Bank and Gaza, thereby denying their Palestinian neighbors a state of their own, is a catastrophe— moral, human, and political—for both peoples. The Palestinians need a sovereign state. Israel needs a sovereign Palestinian state. Those of us abroad who wish for Israel to survive cannot, should not, wish it to survive no matter what, no matter how. We owe a particular debt of gratitude to courageous

Israeli Jewish witnesses, journalists, architects, poets, novelists, professors—among others—who have described and documented and protested and militated against the sufferings of the Palestinians living under the increasingly cruel terms of Israeli military subjugation and settler annexation.

Our greatest admiration must go to the brave Israeli soldiers, represented here by Ishai Menuchin, who refuse to serve beyond the 1967 borders. These soldiers know that all settlements are bound to be evacuated in the end. These soldiers, who are Jews, take seriously the principle put forward at the Nuremberg trials in 1945–46: namely, that a soldier is not obliged to obey unjust orders, orders that contravene the laws of war—indeed, one has an obligation to disobey them.

The Israeli soldiers who are resisting service in the Occupied Territories are not refusing a particular order. They are refusing to enter the space where illegitimate orders are bound to be given—that is, where it is more than probable that they will be ordered to perform actions that continue the oppression and humiliation of Palestinian civilians. Houses are demolished, groves are uprooted, the stalls of a village market are bulldozed, a cultural center is looted; and now, nearly every day, civilians of all ages are fired on and killed. There can be no disputing the mounting cruelty of the Israeli occupation of the twenty-two percent of the former territory of British Palestine on which a Palestinian state will be erected. These soldiers believe, as I do, that there should be an unconditional withdrawal from the Occupied Territories. They have declared collectively that they will not continue to fight beyond the 1967 borders "in order to dominate, expel, starve and humiliate an entire people."

What the refuseniks have done—there are now more

than one thousand of them, more than 250 of whom have gone to prison—does not contribute to tell us how the Israelis and Palestinians can make peace beyond the irrevocable demand that the settlements be disbanded. The actions of this heroic minority cannot contribute to the much-needed reform and democratization of the Palestinian Authority. Their stand will not lessen the grip of religious bigotry and racism in Israeli society or reduce the dissemination of virulent anti-Semitic propaganda in the aggrieved Arab world. It will not stop the suicide bombers.

It simply declares: enough. Or: there is a limit. *Yesh gvul.*

It provides a model of resistance. Of disobedience. For which there will always be penalties.

None of us has yet to endure anything like what these brave conscripts are enduring, many of whom have gone to jail.

To speak for peace at this moment in this country is merely to be jeered (as in the recent Academy Awards ceremony), harassed, blacklisted (the banning by one powerful chain of radio stations of the Dixie Chicks); in short, to be reviled as unpatriotic.

Our "United We Stand" or "Winner Takes All" ethos: the United States is a country that has made patriotism equivalent to consensus. Tocqueville, still the greatest observer of the United States, remarked on an unprecedented degree of conformity in the then-new country, and 168 more years have only confirmed his observation.

Sometimes, given the new, radical turn in American foreign policy, it seems as if it was inevitable that the national consensus on the greatness of America, which may be activated to an extraordinary pitch of triumphalist national self-regard, was bound eventually to find expression in wars like the present one, which are assented to by a majority of the population, who have been persuaded that America has the right—even the duty—to dominate the world.

•

The usual way of heralding people who act on principle is to say that they are the vanguard of an eventually triumphant revolt against injustice.

But what if they're not?

What if the evil is really unstoppable? At least in the short run. And that short run may be—is going to be—very long indeed.

My admiration for the soldiers who are resisting service in the Occupied Territories is as fierce as my belief that it will be a long time before their view prevails.

But what haunts me at this moment—for obvious reasons—is acting on principle when it isn't going to alter the obvious distribution of force, the rank injustice and murderousness of a government policy that claims to be acting in the name not of peace but of security.

The force of arms has its own logic. If you commit an aggression and others resist, it is easy to convince the home front that the fighting must continue. Once the troops are there, they must be supported. It becomes irrelevant to question why the troops are there in the first place.

The soldiers are there because "we" are being attacked or menaced. Never mind that we may have attacked them first. They are now attacking back, causing casualties. Behaving in ways that defy the "proper" conduct of war. Behaving like "savages," as people in our part of the world like to call people in that part of the world. And their "savage" or "unlawful" actions give new justification to new aggressions. And new impetus to repress or censor or persecute citizens who oppose the aggression the government has undertaken.

•

Let's not underestimate the force of what we are opposing.

The world is, for almost everyone, that over which we have virtually no control. Common sense and the sense of self-protectiveness tell us to accommodate to what we cannot change.

It's not hard to see how some of us might be persuaded of the justice, the necessity of a war. Especially of a war that is formulated as small, limited military actions that will actually contribute to peace or improve security; of an aggression that announces itself as a campaign of disarmament— admittedly, disarmament of the enemy; and, regrettably, requiring the application of overpowering force. An invasion that calls itself, officially, a liberation.

Every violence in war has been justified as a retaliation. We are threatened. We are defending ourselves. The others, they want to kill us. We must stop them.

And from there: we must stop them before they have a chance to carry out their plans. And since those who would attack us are sheltering behind noncombatants, no aspect of civil life can be immune to our depredations.

Never mind the disparity of forces, of wealth, of firepower—or simply of population. How many Americans know that the population of Iraq is 24 million, half of whom are children? (The population of the United States, as you will remember, is 290 million.) Not to support those who are coming under fire from the enemy seems like treason.

It may be that, in some cases, the threat is real.

In such circumstances, the bearer of the moral principle seems like someone running alongside a moving train, yelling "Stop! Stop!"

Can the train be stopped? No, it can't. At least, not now.

Will other people on the train be moved to jump off and join those on the ground? Maybe some will, but most won't (at least, not until they have a whole new panoply of fears).

The dramaturgy of "acting on principle" tells us that we don't have to think about whether acting on principle is expedient, or whether we can count on the eventual success of the actions we have undertaken.

Acting on principle is, we're told, a good in itself.

But it is still a political act, in the sense that you're not doing it for yourself. You don't do it just to be in the right, or to appease your own conscience; much less because you are confident your action will achieve its aim. You resist as an act of solidarity. With communities of the principled and the disobedient: here, elsewhere. In the present. In the future.

Thoreau's going to prison in 1846 for refusing to pay the poll tax in protest against the American war on Mexico hardly stopped the war. But the resonance of that most unpunishing and briefest spell of imprisonment (famously, a single night in jail) has not ceased to inspire principled resistance to injustice through the second half of the twentieth century and into our new era. The movement in the late 1980s to shut down the Nevada Test Site, a key location for the nuclear arms race, failed in its goal; the operations of the test site were unaffected by the protests. But it led directly to the formation of a movement of protesters in faraway Alma Ata, who eventually succeeded in shutting down the main Soviet test site in Kazakhstan, citing the Nevada antinuclear activists as their inspiration and expressing solidarity with the Native Americans on whose land the Nevada Test Site had been located.

The likelihood that your acts of resistance cannot stop the injustice does not exempt you from acting in what you sincerely and reflectively hold to be the best interests of your community.

Thus: it is not in the best interests of Israel to be an oppressor.

Thus: it is not in the best interests of the United States to be a hyperpower, capable of imposing its will on any country in the world, as it chooses.

What is in the true interests of a modern community is justice.

It cannot be right to systematically oppress and confine a neighboring people. It is surely false to think that murder, expulsion, annexations, the building of walls—all that has contributed to reducing a whole people to dependence, penury, and despair—will bring security and peace to the oppressors.

It cannot be right that a president of the United States seems to believe that he has a mandate to be president of the planet—and announces that those who are not with America are with "the terrorists."

Those brave Israeli Jews who, in fervent and active opposition to the policies of the present government of their country, have spoken up on behalf of the plight and the rights of Palestinians are defending the true interests of Israel. Those of us who are opposed to the plans of the present government of the United States for global hegemony are patriots speaking for the best interests of the United States.

Beyond these struggles, which are worthy of our passionate adherence, it is important to remember that in programs of political resistance the relation of cause and effect is convoluted and often indirect. All struggle, all resistance is— must be—concrete. And all struggle has a global resonance.

If not here, then there. If not now, then soon. Elsewhere as well as here.

To Archbishop Oscar Arnulfo Romero.

To Rachel Corrie.

And to Ishai Menuchin and his comrades.

Literature Is Freedom

The Friedenspreis Acceptance Speech

President Johannes Rau, Minister of the Interior Otto Schily, State Minister of Culture Christina Weiss, the Lord Mayor of Frankfurt Petra Roth, Vice President of the Bundestag Antje Vollmer, your excellencies, other distinguished guests, honored colleagues, friends . . . among them, dear Ivan Nagel:

To speak in the Paulskirche, before this audience, to receive the prize awarded in the last fifty-three years by the German Book Trade to so many writers, thinkers, and exemplary public figures whom I admire—to speak, as I say, in this history-charged place and on this occasion, is a humbling and inspiring experience. I can only the more regret the deliberate absence of the American ambassador, Mr. Daniel Coats, whose immediate refusal, in June, of the invitation from the Book Trade, when this year's Friedenspreis was announced, to attend our gathering here today, shows he is more interested in affirming the ideological stance and the rancorous reactiveness of the Bush administration than he is, by fulfilling a normal diplomatic duty, in representing the interests and reputation of his—and my—country.

Ambassador Coats has chosen not to be here, I assume, because of criticisms I have voiced, in newspaper and television interviews and in brief magazine articles, of the new radical bent of American foreign policy, as exemplified by the invasion and occupation of Iraq. He should be here, I think, because a citizen of the country he represents in Germany has been honored with an important German prize.

An American ambassador has the duty to represent his country, all of it. I, of course, do not represent America, not even that substantial minority that does not support the imperial program of Mr. Bush and his advisers. I like to think I do not represent anything but literature, a certain idea of literature, and conscience, a certain idea of conscience or duty, but, mindful of the citation for this prize from a major European country, which mentions my role as an "intellectual ambassador" between the two continents (ambassador, needless to say, in the weakest, merely metaphorical sense), I cannot resist offering a few thoughts about the renowned gap between Europe and the United States, which my interests and enthusiasms purportedly bridge.

First, is it a gap—that continues to be bridged? Or is it not also a conflict? Irate, dismissive statements about Europe, certain European countries, are now the common coin of American political rhetoric; and here, at least in the rich countries on the western side of the continent, anti-American sentiments are more common, more audible, more intemperate than ever. What is this conflict? Does it have deep roots? I think it does.

There has always been a latent antagonism between Europe and America, one at least as complex and ambivalent as that between parent and child. America is a neo-European country and, until the last few decades, was largely populated by European peoples. And yet it is always the differences between Europe and America that have struck the most perceptive European observers: Alexis de Tocqueville, who visited the young nation in 1831 and returned to France to write *Democracy in America*, still, some 170 years later, the best book about my country, and D. H. Lawrence, who, eighty years ago, published the most interesting book ever written about American culture, his influential, exasperating *Studies in Classic American Literature*, both understood that America, the child of Europe, was becoming, or had become, the antithesis of Europe.

Rome and Athens. Mars and Venus. The authors of recent popular tracts promoting the idea of an inevitable clash of interests and values between Europe and America did not invent these antitheses. Foreigners brooded over them—and they provide the palette, the recurrent melody, in much of American literature throughout the nineteenth century, from James Fenimore Cooper and Ralph Waldo Emerson to Walt Whitman, Henry James, William Dean Howells, and Mark Twain. American innocence and European sophistication; American pragmatism and European intellectualizing; American energy and European world-weariness; American naïveté and European cynicism; American good-heartedness and European malice; American moralism and the European arts of compromise—you know the tunes.

You can choreograph them differently; indeed, they have been danced with every kind of evaluation or tilt for two

tumultuous centuries. Europhiles can use the venerable antitheses to identify America with commerce-driven barbarism
and Europe with high culture, while the Europhobes draw on a
ready-made view in which America stands for idealism and
openness and democracy and Europe a debilitating, snobbish
refinement. Tocqueville and Lawrence observed something
fiercer: not just a declaration of independence from Europe,
and European values, but a steady undermining, an assassination, of European values and European power. "You can never
have a new thing without breaking an old," Lawrence wrote.
"Europe happened to be the old thing. America . . . should be
the new thing. The new thing is the death of the old." America, Lawrence divined, was on a Europe-destroying mission,
using democracy—particularly cultural democracy, democracy
of manners—as an instrument. And when that task is accomplished, he went on, America might well turn from
democracy to something else. (What that might be is, perhaps, emerging now.)

Bear with me if my references have been exclusively literary. After all, one function of literature—of important literature, of necessary literature—is to be prophetic. What we
have here, writ large, is the perennial literary—or cultural—
quarrel: between the ancients and the moderns.

The past is (or was) Europe, and America was founded
on the idea of breaking with the past, which is viewed as
encumbering, stultifying, and—in its forms of deference
and precedence, its standards of what is superior and what is
best—fundamentally undemocratic; or "elitist," the reigning
current synonym. Those who speak for a triumphal America
continue to intimate that American democracy implies re-
pudiating Europe and, yes, embracing a certain liberating,

salutary barbarism. If, today, Europe is regarded by most Americans as more socialist than elitist, that still makes Europe, by American standards, a retrograde continent, obstinately attached to old standards: the welfare state. "Make it new" is not only a slogan for culture; it describes an ever-advancing, world-encompassing economic machine.

However, if necessary, even the "old" can be rebaptized as the "new."

It is not a coincidence that the strong-minded American secretary of defense tried to drive a wedge within Europe—distinguishing unforgettably between an "old" Europe (bad) and a "new" Europe (good). How did Germany, France, and Belgium come to be consigned to "old" Europe, while Spain, Italy, Poland, Ukraine, the Netherlands, Hungary, the Czech Republic, and Bulgaria find themselves part of "new" Europe? Answer: to support the United States in its present extensions of political and military power is, by definition, to pass into the more desirable category of the "new." Whoever is with us is "new."

All modern wars, even when their aims are the traditional ones, such as territorial aggrandizement or the acquisition of scarce resources, are cast as clashes of civilizations—culture wars—with each side claiming the high ground and characterizing the other as barbaric. The enemy is invariably a threat to "our way of life," an infidel, a desecrator, a polluter, a defiler of higher or better values. The current war against the very real threat posed by militant Islamic fundamentalism is a particularly clear example. What is worth remarking is that a milder version of the same terms of disparagement underlies the antagonism between Europe and America. It should also be remembered that, historically, the most virulent anti-American rhetoric ever heard in Europe—consisting essentially in the charge that Americans are barbarians—came not from the so-called left but from the extreme right. Both Hitler and Franco repeatedly inveighed against an America (and a world Jewry) engaged in polluting European civilization with its base business values.

Of course, much of European public opinion continues to admire American energy, the American version of "the modern." And to be sure, there have always been American fellow-travelers of the European cultural ideals (one stands here before you), who find in the old arts of Europe correction and a liberation from the strenuous mercantilist biases of American culture. And there have always been the counterparts of such Americans: Europeans who are fascinated, enthralled, profoundly attracted to the United States, precisely because of its difference from Europe.

What the Americans see is almost the reverse of the Europhile cliché: they see themselves defending civilization. The barbarian hordes are no longer outside the gates. They are within, in every prosperous city, plotting havoc. The "chocolate-producing" countries (France, Germany, Belgium) will have to stand aside, while a country with "will"—and God on its side—pursues the battle against terrorism (now conflated with barbarism). According to Secretary of State Colin Powell, it is ridiculous for "old" Europe (sometimes it seems only France is meant) to aspire to play a role in governing or administering the territories won by the coalition of the conqueror. It has neither the military resources nor the taste for violence nor the support of its cosseted, all-too-pacific populations. And the Americans have it right. Europeans are not in an evangelical—or a bellicose—mood.

Indeed, sometimes I have to pinch myself to be sure I am not dreaming: that what many people in my own country now hold against Germany, which wreaked such horrors on the world for nearly a century—the new "German problem," as it were—is that Germans are repelled by war; that much of German public opinion is now virtually pacifist!

Were America and Europe never partners, never friends? Of course. But perhaps it is true that the periods of unity—of common feeling—have been exceptions rather than the rule. One such time was from the Second World War through the early Cold War, when Europeans were profoundly grateful for America's intervention, succor, and support. Americans are comfortable seeing themselves in the role of Europe's savior. But then America will expect the Europeans to be forever grateful, which is not what Europeans are feeling right now. From "old" Europe's point of view, America seems bent on squandering the admiration—and gratitude—felt by most Europeans. The immense sympathy for the United States in the aftermath of the attack on September 11, 2001, was genuine. (I can testify to its resounding ardor and sincerity in Germany; I was in Berlin at the time.) But what has followed is an increasing estrangement on both sides.

The citizens of the richest and most powerful nation in history have to know that America is loved and envied . . . and resented. More than a few who travel abroad know that Americans are regarded as crude, boorish, uncultivated by many Europeans, and don't hesitate to match these expectations with behavior that suggests the *ressentiment* of excolonials. And some of the cultivated Europeans who seem most to enjoy visiting or living in the United States attribute to it, condescendingly, the liberating ambiance of a colony where one can throw off the restrictions and high-culture burdens of "back home." I recall being told by a German filmmaker, living at the time in San Francisco, that he loved being in the States "because you don't have any culture here." For more than a few Europeans, including, it should be mentioned, D. H. Lawrence ("There the life comes up from the roots, crude but vital," he wrote to a friend in 1915, when he was making plans to live in America), America was the great escape. And vice versa: Europe was the great escape for generations of Americans seeking "culture." Of course, I am speaking only of minorities here, minorities of the privileged.

So America now sees itself as the defender of civilization and Europe's savior and wonders why Europeans don't get the point; and Europeans see America as a reckless warrior state—a description that the Americans return by seeing Europe as the enemy of America: only pretending, so runs rhetoric heard increasingly in the United States, to be pacifist, in order to contribute to the weakening of American power. France in particular is thought to be scheming to become America's equal, even its superior, in shaping world affairs—"Operation America Must Fail" is the name invented by a columnist in *The New York Times* to describe the French drive toward dominance—instead of realizing that an American defeat in Iraq will (in the words of the same columnist) encourage "radical Muslim groups—from Baghdad to the Muslim slums of Paris" to pursue their jihad against tolerance and democracy.

It is hard for people not to see the world in polarizing terms ("them" and "us"), and these terms have in the past strengthened the isolationist theme in American foreign policy as much as they now strengthen the imperialist theme. Americans have got used to thinking of the world in terms of enemies. Enemies are somewhere else, as the fighting is almost always "over there," with Islamic fundamentalism now replacing Russian and Chinese Communism as the implacable, furtive menace. And "terrorist" is a more flexible word than "Communist." It can unify a larger number of quite different struggles and interests. What this may mean is that the war will be endless—since there will always be some terrorism (as there will always be poverty and cancer); that is, there will always be asymmetrical conflicts in which the weaker side uses that form of violence, which usually targets civilians. American rhetoric, which doesn't necessarily coincide with public opinion, would support this unfortunate prospect, for the struggle for righteousness never ends.

It is the genius of the United States, a profoundly conservative country in ways that Europeans find difficult to fathom, to have elaborated a form of conservative thinking that celebrates the new rather than the old. But this is also to say that in the very ways in which the United States seems extremely conservative—for example, the extraordinary power of the consensus and the passivity and conformism of public opinion (as Tocqueville remarked in 1831) and the media—it is also radical, even revolutionary, in ways that Europeans find equally difficult to fathom.

Part of the puzzle, surely, lies in the disconnect between official rhetoric and lived realities. Americans are constantly extolling "traditions"; litanies to family values are at the center of every politician's discourse. And yet the culture of America is extremely corrosive of family life, indeed of all traditions except those redefined as "identities" that fit into the larger patterns of distinctiveness, cooperation, and openness to innovation.

Perhaps the most important source of the new (and not so new) American radicalism is what used to be viewed as a source of conservative values: namely, religion. Many commentators have noted that perhaps the biggest difference between the United States and most European countries (old as well as new, according to the current American distinction) is that in the United States religion still plays a central role in society and public language. But this is religion American style: more the idea of religion than religion itself.

True, when, during George Bush's run for president in 2000, a journalist was inspired to ask the candidate to name his "favorite philosopher," the well-received answer—one that would make a candidate for high office from any centrist party in any European country a laughingstock—was "Jesus Christ." But of course, Bush didn't mean, and was not understood to mean, that, if elected, his administration would actually feel bound by any of the precepts or social programs expounded by Jesus.

The United States is a generically religious society. That is, in the United States it's not important which religion you adhere to, as long as you have one. To have a ruling religion, even a theocracy, that would be just Christian (or a particular Christian denomination) would be impossible. Religion in America must be a matter of choice. This modern, relatively contentless idea of religion, constructed along the lines of consumerist choice, is the basis of American conformism, self-righteousness, and moralism (which Europeans often mistake, condescendingly, for Puritanism). Whatever historic faiths the different American religious entities purport to represent, they all preach something similar: reform of personal behavior, the value of success, community cooperativeness, tolerance of others' choices (all virtues that further and smooth the functioning of consumer capitalism). The very fact of being religious ensures respectability, promotes order, and gives the guarantee of virtuous intentions to the mission of the United States to lead the world.

What is being spread—whether it is called democracy, or freedom, or civilization—is part of a work in progress, as well as the essence of progress itself. Nowhere in the world does the Enlightenment dream of progress have such a fertile setting as it does in America.

·

Are we then really so separate? How odd that, at a moment when Europe and America have never been so similar culturally, there has never been such a great divide.

Still, for all the similarities in the daily lives of citizens in rich European countries and the daily lives of Americans, the gap between the European and the American experience is a genuine one, founded on important differences of history, of notions of the role of culture, of real and imagined memories. The antagonism—for there is antagonism—is not to be resolved in the immediate future, for all the goodwill of many people on both sides of the Atlantic. And yet one can only deplore those who want to maximize those differences, when we do have so much in common.

The dominance of America is a fact. But America, as the present administration is starting to see, cannot do everything alone. The future of our world—the world we share—is syncretistic, impure. We are not shut off from each other. More and more we leak into each other.

In the end, the model for whatever understanding— conciliation—we might reach lies in thinking more about that venerable opposition, "old" and "new." The opposition between "civilization" and "barbarism" is essentially stipulatory; it is corrupting to think about and pontificate about— however much it may reflect certain undeniable realities. But the opposition of "old" and "new" is genuine, ineradicable, at the center of what we understand to be experience itself.

"Old" and "new" are the perennial poles of all feeling and sense of orientation in the world. We cannot do without the old, because in what is old is invested all our past, our wisdom, our memories, our sadness, our sense of realism. We cannot do without faith in the new, because in what is new is invested all our energy, our capacity for optimism, our blind biological yearning, our ability to forget—the healing ability that makes reconciliation possible.

The inner life tends to mistrust the new. A strongly developed inner life will be particularly resistant to the new. We are told we must choose—the old or the new. In fact, we must choose both. What is a life if not a series of negotiations between the old and the new? It seems to me that one should always be seeking to talk oneself out of these stark oppositions.

Old versus new, nature versus culture—perhaps it is inevitable that the great myths of our cultural life be played out as geography, not only as history. Still, they are myths, clichés, stereotypes, no more; the realities are much more complex.

A good deal of my life has been devoted to trying to demystify ways of thinking that polarize and oppose. Translated into politics, this means favoring what is pluralistic and secular. Like some Americans and many Europeans, I would far prefer to live in a multilateral world—a world not dominated by any one country (including my own). I could express my support, in a century that already promises to be another century of extremes, of horrors, for a whole panoply of meliorist principles—in particular, for what Virginia Woolf calls "the melancholy virtue of tolerance."

Let me rather speak first of all as a writer, as a champion of the enterprise of literature, for therein lies the only authority I have.

The writer in me distrusts the good citizen, the "intellectual ambassador," the human rights activist—those roles which are mentioned in the citation for this prize, much as I am committed to them. The writer is more skeptical, more self-doubting, than the person who tries to do (and to support) the right thing.

One task of literature is to formulate questions and construct counterstatements to the reigning pieties. And even when art is not oppositional, the arts gravitate toward contrariness. Literature is dialogue; responsiveness. Literature might be described as the history of human responsiveness to what is alive and what is moribund as cultures evolve and interact with one another.

Writers can do something to combat these clichés of our separateness, our difference—for writers are makers, not just transmitters, of myths. Literature offers not only myths but countermyths, just as life offers counterexperiences— experiences that confound what you thought you thought, or felt, or believed.

A writer, I think, is someone who pays attention to the world. That means trying to understand, take in, connect with, what wickedness human beings are capable of; and

not be corrupted—made cynical, superficial—by this understanding.

Literature can tell us what the world is like.

Literature can give standards and pass on deep knowledge, incarnated in language, in narrative.

Literature can train, and exercise, our ability to weep for
those who are not us or ours.

Who would we be if we could not sympathize with those
who are not us or ours? Who would we be if we could not forget ourselves, at least some of the time? Who would we be if
we could not learn? Forgive? Become something other than
we are?

.

On the occasion of receiving this glorious prize, this
glorious German prize, let me tell you something of my own
trajectory.

I was born, a third-generation American of Polish and
Lithuanian Jewish descent, two weeks before Hitler came to
power. I grew up in the American provinces (Arizona and California), far from Germany, and yet my entire childhood was
haunted by Germany, by the monstrousness of Germany, and
by the German books and the German music I loved, which
set my standard for what is exalted and intense.

Even before Bach and Mozart and Beethoven and Schu-
bert and Brahms, there were a few German books. I am thinking of a teacher in an elementary school in a small town in
southern Arizona, Mr. Starkie, who had awed his pupils by
telling us that he had fought with Pershing's army in Mexico
against Pancho Villa: this grizzled veteran of an earlier American imperialist venture had, it seems, been touched—in

translation—by the idealism of German literature and, having taken in my particular hunger for books, loaned me his own copies of *The Sorrows of Young Werther* and *Immensee*.

Soon after, in my childhood orgy of reading, chance led me to other German books, including Kafka's *In the Penal Colony*, where I discovered dread and injustice. And a few years later, when I was a high school student in Los Angeles, I found all of Europe in a German novel. No book has been more important in my life than *The Magic Mountain*—whose subject is, precisely, the clash of ideals at the heart of European civilization. And so on, through a long life that has been steeped in German high culture. Indeed, after the books and the music, which were, given the cultural desert in which I lived, virtually clandestine experiences, came real experiences. For I am also a late beneficiary of the German cultural diaspora, having had the great good fortune of knowing well some of the incomparably brilliant Hitler refugees, those writers and artists and musicians and scholars that America received in the 1930s and who so enriched the country, particularly its universities. Let me name two I was privileged to count as friends when I was in my late teens and early twenties, Hans Gerth and Herbert Marcuse; those with whom I studied at the University of Chicago and at Harvard, Christian Mackauer and Leo Strauss and Paul Tillich and Peter Heinrich von Blanckenhagen, and in private seminars, Aron Gurwitsch and Nahum Glatzer; and Hannah Arendt, whom I knew after I moved to New York in my mid-twenties—so many models of the serious, whose memory I would like to evoke here.

But I shall never forget that my engagement with German culture, with German seriousness, all started with obscure, eccentric Mr. Starkie (I don't think I ever knew his first name), who was my teacher when I was ten and whom I never saw afterward.

And that brings me to a story, with which I will conclude—as seems fitting, since I am primarily neither a cultural ambassador nor a fervent critic of my own government (a task I perform as a good American citizen). I am a storyteller.

So, back to ten-year-old me, who found some relief from the tiresome duties of being a child by poring over Mr. Starkie's tattered volumes of Goethe and Storm. At the time I am speaking of, 1943, I was aware that there was a prison camp with thousands of German soldiers—Nazi soldiers, as of course I thought of them—in the northern part of the state, and knowing I was Jewish (if only nominally, my family having been completely secular and assimilated for two generations; nominally, I knew, was enough for Nazis), I was beset by a recurrent nightmare in which Nazi soldiers had escaped from the prison and had made their way downstate to the bungalow on the outskirts of the town where I lived with my mother and sister and were about to kill me.

Flash-forward to many years later, the 1970s, when my books started to be published by Hanser Verlag, and I came to know the distinguished Fritz Arnold (he had joined the firm in 1965), who was my editor at Hanser until his death in February 1999.

One of the first times we were together, Fritz said he wanted to tell me—presuming, I suppose, that this was a prerequisite to any friendship that might arise between us— what he had done during the war. I assured him that he did not owe me any such explanation; but of course, I was touched

by his bringing up the subject. I should add that Fritz Arnold
was not the only German of his generation (he was born in
1916) who, soon after we met, insisted on telling me what he
or she had done in Nazi times. And not all of the stories were
as innocent as what I was to hear from Fritz.

Anyway, what Fritz told me was that he had been a university student of literature and art history, first in Munich,
then in Cologne, when, at the start of the war, he was drafted
into the Wehrmacht with the rank of corporal. His family
was, of course, anything but pro-Nazi—his father was Karl
Arnold, the legendary political cartoonist of *Simplicissimus*—
but emigration seemed out of the question, and he accepted,
with dread, the call to military service, hoping neither to kill
anyone nor to be killed.

Fritz was one of the lucky ones. Lucky to have been sta-
tioned first in Rome (where he refused his superior officer's
invitation to be commissioned a lieutenant), then in Tunis;
lucky enough to have remained behind the lines and never
once to have fired a weapon; and finally, lucky, if that is the
right word, to have been taken prisoner by the Americans in
1943, to have been transported by ship across the Atlantic
with other captured German soldiers to Norfolk, Virginia,
and then taken by train across the continent to spend the rest
of the war in a prison camp in . . . northern Arizona.

Then I had the pleasure of telling him, sighing with
wonder, for I had already started to be very fond of this
man—this was the beginning of a great friendship as well
as an intense professional relationship—that while he was a
prisoner of war in northern Arizona, I was in the southern
part of the state, terrified of the Nazi soldiers who were there,
here, and from whom there would be no escape.

And then Fritz told me that what got him through his nearly three years in the prison camp in Arizona was that he was allowed access to books: he had spent those years reading and rereading the English and American classics. And I told him that what saved me as a schoolchild in Arizona, waiting to grow up, waiting to escape into a larger reality, was reading books, books in translation as well as those written in English.

To have access to literature, world literature, was to escape the prison of national vanity, of philistinism, of compulsory provincialism, of inane schooling, of imperfect destinies and bad luck. Literature was the passport to enter a larger life; that is, the zone of freedom.

Literature was freedom. Especially in a time in which the values of reading and inwardness are so strenuously challenged, literature *is* freedom.

At the Same Time:
The Novelist and Moral
Reasoning

The Nadine Gordimer Lecture

Long ago—it was the eighteenth century—a great and eccentric defender of literature and the English language—it was Doctor Johnson—wrote, in the preface to his *Dictionary*: "The chief glory of every people arises from its authors."

An unconventional proposition, I suspect, even then. And far more unconventional now, though I think it's still true. Even at the beginning of the twenty-first century. Of course, I am speaking of the glory that is permanent, not transitory.

I'm often asked if there is something I think writers *ought* to do, and recently in an interview I heard myself say: "Several things. Love words, agonize over sentences. And pay attention to the world."

Needless to say, no sooner had these perky phrases fallen out of my mouth than I thought of some more recipes for writer's virtue.

For instance: "Be serious." By which I meant: Never be cynical. And which *doesn't* preclude being funny.

And . . . if you'll allow me one more: "Take care to be born at a time when it was *likely* that you would be definitively exalted and influenced by Dostoyevsky, and Tolstoy, and Turgenev, and Chekhov."

The truth is, whatever it might occur to you to say about what a writer *ideally* should be, there is always something more. All these descriptions mean nothing without examples. So if asked to name a living writer who exemplifies all that a writer can be, I would think immediately of Nadine Gordimer.

A great writer of fiction both *creates*—through acts of imagination, through language that feels inevitable, through vivid forms—a new world, a world that is unique, individual; and *responds* to a world, the world the writer shares with other people but is unknown or mis-known by still more people, confined in *their* worlds: call *that* history, society, what you will.

Nadine Gordimer's large, ravishingly eloquent, and extremely varied body of work is, first of all, a treasury of human beings *in situations*, stories that are character-driven. Her books have brought us her imagination, which is now part of the imagination of her many readers everywhere. In particular, they have brought to those of us who are not South African a wide, wide portrait of the part of the world of which she is native and to which she has paid such exacting, responsible attention.

Her exemplary, influential stand in the decades-long revolutionary struggle for justice and equality in South Africa, her natural sympathy for comparable struggles elsewhere in the world—these have been justly celebrated. Few first-rank writers today have fulfilled the multiple ethical tasks available to a writer of conscience and great intellectual gifts as whole-heartedly, as energetically, as bravely as has Nadine Gordimer.

But of course, the primary task of a writer is to write well. (And to go on writing well. Neither to burn out nor to sell out.) In the end—that is to say, from the point of view of literature—Nadine Gordimer is not representative of any-body or anything but herself. That, and the noble cause of literature.

Let the dedicated activist never overshadow the dedi-cated servant of literature—the matchless storyteller.

To write is to know something. What a pleasure to read a writer who knows a great deal. (Not a common experience these days . . .) Literature, I would argue, *is* knowledge—albeit, even at its greatest, imperfect knowledge. Like *all* knowledge.

Still, even now, even now, literature remains one of our principal modes of understanding. And Nadine Gordimer un-derstands a great deal about the private life—about family bonds; family affections; the powers of eros—and about the contradictory demands that struggles in the public arena can make on the serious writer.

Everybody in our debauched culture invites us to *sim-plify* reality, to *despise* wisdom. There is a great deal of wis-dom in Nadine Gordimer's work. She has articulated an admirably complex view of the human heart and the contra-dictions inherent in living in literature and in history.

•

It is a singular honor to be invited to give the first Nadine Gordimer Lecture and to have the occasion—this wonderful occasion—to pay tribute to what her work has

meant to me, to us all, in its lucidity and passion and elo-
quence and fidelity to the idea of the *responsibility* of the
writer to literature and to society.

By literature, I mean literature in the normative sense,
the sense in which literature incarnates and defends high
standards. By society, I mean society in the normative sense,
too—which suggests that a great writer of fiction, by writing
truthfully about the society in which she or he lives, cannot
help but evoke (if only by their absence) the better standards
of justice and of truthfulness that we have the right (some
would say the duty) to militate for in the necessarily imperfect societies in which we live.

Obviously, I think of the writer of novels and stories and
plays as a moral agent. Indeed, this conception of the writer is
one of the many links between Nadine Gordimer's idea of
literature and mine. In my view, and I believe in Nadine
Gordimer's, a fiction writer whose adherence is to literature
is, necessarily, someone who thinks about moral problems:
about what is just and unjust, what is better or worse, what is
repulsive and admirable, what is lamentable and what inspires joy and approbation. This doesn't entail moralizing in
any direct or crude sense. Serious fiction writers think about
moral problems *practically*. They tell stories. They narrate.
They evoke our common humanity in narratives with which
we can identify, even though the lives may be remote from
our own. They stimulate our imagination. The stories they
tell enlarge and complicate—and, therefore, improve—our
sympathies. They educate our capacity for moral judgment.

When I say the fiction writer narrates, I mean that the
story has a shape: a beginning, a middle (properly called a development), and an end or resolution. Every writer of fiction

wants to tell many stories, but we know that we can't tell *all* the stories—certainly not simultaneously. We know we must pick one story, well, one *central* story; we have to be selective. The art of the writer is to find as much as one can in that story, in that sequence . . . in *that* time (the timeline of the story), in *that* space (the concrete geography of the story). "There are so many stories to tell," muses the alter ego voice in the monologue that opens my last novel, *In America.* "There are so many stories to tell, it's hard to say why it's one rather than another, it must be because with this story you feel you can tell many stories, that there will be a necessity in it; I see I am explaining badly . . . It has to be something like falling in love. Whatever explains why you chose this story . . . hasn't explained much. A story, I mean a long story, a novel, is like an around-the-world-in-eighty-days: you can barely recall the beginning when it comes to an end."

A novelist, then, is someone who takes you on a journey. Through space. Through time. A novelist leads the reader over a gap, makes something go where it was not.

•

There is an old riff I've always imagined to have been invented by some graduate student of philosophy (as I was once myself), late one night, who had been struggling through Kant's abstruse account in his *Critique of Pure Reason* of the barely comprehensible categories of time and space, and decided that all of this could be put much more simply.

It goes as follows:

"Time exists in order that everything doesn't happen all at once . . . and space exists so that it doesn't all happen to you."

By this standard, the novel is an ideal vehicle both of space and of time. The novel shows us time: that is, everything doesn't happen at once. (It is a sequence, it is a line.) It shows us space: that is, what happens doesn't happen to one person only.

In other words, a novel is the creation not simply of a voice but of a world. It mimics the essential structures by which we experience ourselves as living in time, and inhabiting a world, and attempting to make sense of our experience. But it does what lives (the lives that are lived) *cannot* offer, except after they are over. It confers—and withdraws—meaning or sense upon a life. This is possible because narration is possible, because there are norms of narration that are as constitutive of thinking and feeling and experiencing as are, in the Kantian account, the mental categories of space and time.

A *spacious* way of conceiving human action is an intrinsic feature of the novelist's imagination, even when the point of a given fiction is precisely to affirm the impossibility of a genuinely spacious world, as in the claustrophobic narratives of Samuel Beckett and Thomas Bernhard.

A conviction of the potential richness of our existence *in time* is also characteristic of the imagination that is distinctively novelistic, even when the novelist's point—again one could cite Beckett and Bernhard—is to illustrate the futility and repetitiousness of action in time. Like the world in which we actually live, the worlds that novelists create possess both a history and a geography. They would not be novels if they did not.

In other words—and once again—the novel tells a story. I don't mean only that the story is the content of the novel, which is then deployed or organized into a literary narrative according to various ideas of form. I am arguing that having a story to tell is the chief *formal* property of a novel; and that the novelist, whatever the complexity of his or her means, is bound by—liberated by—the fundamental logic of storytelling.

The essential scheme of storytelling is linear (even when it is antichronological). It proceeds from a "before" (or: "at first") to a "during" to a "finally" or "after." But this is much more than mere causal sequence, just as lived time—which distends with feeling and contracts with the deadening of feeling—is not uniform, clock time. The work of the novelist is to enliven time, as it is to animate space.

The dimension of time is essential for prose fiction, but not, if I may invoke the old idea of the two-party system in literature, for poetry (that is, lyric poetry). Poetry is situated in the present. Poems, even when they tell stories, are not *like* stories.

One difference lies in the role of metaphor, which, I would argue, is *necessary* in poetry. Indeed, in my view, it is the task—one of the tasks—of the poet to invent metaphors. One of the fundamental resources of human understanding is what could be called the "pictural" sense, which is secured by comparing one thing with another. Here are some venerable examples, familiar (and plausible) to everyone:

time as river flowing
life as dream
death as sleep
love as illness
life as play/stage
wisdom as light
eyes as stars

book as world
human being as tree
music as food
etc., etc.

A great poet is one who refines and elaborates the great historical store of metaphors and adds to our stock of metaphors. Metaphors offer a profound form of understanding, and many—but hardly all—novelists have recourse to metaphor. The grasp of experience through metaphor is not the *distinctive* understanding that is offered by the great novelists. Virginia Woolf is not a greater novelist than Thomas Bernhard because she uses metaphors and he does not.

The understanding of the novelist is temporal, rather than spatial or pictural. Its medium is a rendered sense of time—time experienced as an arena of struggle or conflict or choice. All stories are about battles, struggles of one kind or another, that terminate in victory and in defeat. Everything moves toward the end, when the outcome will be known.

•

"The modern" is an idea, a very radical idea, that continues to evolve. We are now in a second phase of the ideology of the modern (which has been given the presumptuous name of "the postmodern").

In literature, the modern is generally traced back to Flaubert, the first totally self-conscious novelist, who seemed modern, or advanced, because he worried about his prose, judging it by rigorous standards—such as velocity, economy, precision, density—that seemed to echo anxieties hitherto confined to the domain of poetry.

Flaubert also heralded the turn toward "abstraction" characteristic of the modern strategies in making and defending art by denying the primacy of subject matter. He once described *Madame Bovary*, a novel with a classically shaped story and subject matter, as being about the color brown. Another time Flaubert said it was about . . . nothing.

Of course, nobody thought that *Madame Bovary* was really about the color brown or about "nothing." What is exemplary is the extent of the writerly scrupulousness—perfectionism, if you will—implied by such patent hyperbole. Of Flaubert, one could echo what Picasso remarked about Cézanne: what attaches every serious novelist to Flaubert is, even more than his achievement, his anxiety.

This beginning of "the modern" in literature took place in the 1850s. A century and a half is a long time. Many of the attitudes and scruples and refusals associated with "the modern" in literature—as well as in the other arts—have begun to seem conventional or even sterile. And, to some extent, this judgment is justified. Every notion of literature, even the most exacting and liberating, can become a form of spiritual complacency or self-congratulation.

Most notions about literature are reactive—in the hands of lesser talents, merely reactive. But what is happening in the repudiations advanced in the current debate about the novel goes far beyond the usual process whereby new talents need to repudiate older ideas of literary excellence.

In North America and in Europe, we are living now, I think it fair to say, in a period of *reaction*. In the arts, it takes the form of a bullying reaction against the high modernist achievement, which is thought to be too difficult, too demanding of audiences, not accessible (or "user-friendly") enough.

And in politics, it takes the form of a dismissal of all attempts to measure public life by what are disparaged as mere ideals.

In the modern era, the call for a return to realism in the arts often goes hand in hand with the strengthening of cynical realism in political discourse.

The greatest offense now, in matters both of the arts and of culture generally, not to mention political life, is to seem to be upholding some better, more exigent standard, which is attacked, both from the left and the right, as either naïve or (a new banner for the philistines) "elitist."

Proclamations about the death of the novel—or in its newer form, the end of books—have, of course, been a staple of the debate about literature for almost a century. But they have recently attained a new virulence and theoretical persuasiveness.

Ever since word-processing programs became commonplace tools for most writers—including me—there have been those who assert that there is now a brave new future for fiction.

The argument goes as follows.

The novel, as we know it, has come to its end. However, there is no cause for lament. Something better (and more democratic) is going to replace it: the hypernovel, which will be written in the nonlinear or nonsequential space made possible by the computer.

This new model for fiction proposes to liberate the reader from the two mainstays of the traditional novel: linear narrative and the author. The reader, cruelly forced to read one word after another to reach the end of a *sentence*, one paragraph after another to reach the end of a *scene*, will rejoice to learn that, according to one account, "true freedom" for the reader is now possible, thanks to the advent of the computer: "freedom from the tyranny of the line." A hypernovel "has no beginning; it is reversible; we gain access to it by several entrances, none of which can be authoritatively declared to be the main one." Instead of following a linear story dictated by the author, the reader can now navigate at will through an "endless expansion of words."

I think most readers—surely, virtually *all* readers—will be surprised to learn that structured storytelling—from the most basic beginning-middle-end scheme of traditional tales to more elaborately constructed, nonchronological and multivoiced narratives—is actually a form of oppression rather than a source of delight.

In fact, what interests most readers about fiction is precisely the story—whether in fairy tales, in murder mysteries, or in the complex narratives of Cervantes and Dostoyevsky and Jane Austen and Proust and Italo Calvino. Story—the idea that events happen in a specific causal order—is both the way we see the world and what interests us most about it. People who read for nothing else will read for plot.

Yet hyperfiction's advocates maintain that we find plot "confining" and chafe against its limitations. That we resent and long to be liberated from the age-old tyranny of the author, who dictates how the story will turn out, and wish to be truly active readers, who at any moment in reading the text can choose between various alternative continuations or outcomes of the story by rearranging its blocks of text. Hyperfiction is sometimes said to mimic real life, with its myriad opportunities and surprising outcomes, so I suppose it is being touted as a kind of ultimate realism.

To this, I would answer that, while it is true that we expect to organize and make sense of our lives, we do not expect to write other people's novels for them. And one of the resources we have for helping us to make sense of our lives, and make choices, and propose and accept standards for ourselves, is our experience of *singular* authoritative voices, not our own, which make up that great body of work that educates the heart and the feelings and teaches us to be in the world, that embodies and defends the glories of language (that is, expands the basic instrument of consciousness): namely, *literature*.

What is more true is that the hypertext—or should I say the ideology of hypertext?—is ultrademocratic and so entirely in harmony with the demagogic appeals to cultural democracy that accompany (and distract one's attention from) the ever-tightening grip of plutocratic capitalism.

This proposal that the novel of the future will have *no* story or, instead, a story of the reader's (rather, *readers'*) devising is so plainly unappealing and, should it come to pass, would inevitably bring about not the much-heralded death of the author but the extinction of the reader—*all* future readers of what is labeled as "literature." It's easy to see that it could only have been an invention of *academic* literary criticism, which has been overwhelmed by a plethora of notions expressing the keenest hostility to the very project of literature itself.

But there is more to the idea than that.

These proclamations that the book and the novel in particular are ending can't simply be ascribed to the mischief wreaked by the ideology that has come to dominate departments of literature in many major universities in the United States, Great Britain, and Western Europe. (I don't know how

true this is of South Africa.) The real force behind the argument against literature, against the book, comes, I think, from
the hegemony of the narrative model proposed by television.

•

A novel is *not* a set of proposals, or a list, or a collection
of agendas, or an (open-ended, revisable) itinerary. It is the
journey itself—made, experienced, and completed.

Completion does not mean that everything has been
told. Henry James, as he was coming to the end of writing
one of his greatest novels, *The Portrait of a Lady*, confided to
himself in his notebook his worry that his readers would
think that the novel was not really finished, that he had "not
seen the heroine to the end of her situation." (As you will
remember, James leaves his heroine, the brilliant and ideal-
istic Isabel Archer, resolved *not* to leave her husband, whom
she has discovered to be a mercenary scoundrel, though
there is a former suitor, the aptly named Caspar Goodwood,
who, still in love with her, hopes she will change her mind.)
But, James argued to himself, his novel would be rightly finished on this note. As he wrote: "The *whole* of anything is
never told; you can only take what groups together. What I
have done has that unity—it groups together. It is complete
in itself."

We, James's readers, may wish that Isabel Archer would
leave her dreadful husband for happiness with loving, faithful, honorable Caspar Goodwood: I certainly wish she would.
But James is telling us she will not.

Every fictional plot contains hints and traces of the stories it has excluded or resisted in order to assume its present

shape. Alternatives to the plot ought to be felt up to the last moment. These alternatives constitute the potential for disorder (and therefore of suspense) in the story's unfolding.

The pressure for events to turn out differently lies behind every unfortunate reversal, every new challenge to a stable outcome. Readers count on such lines of resistance to keep the narrative unsettled, permeated with the threat of further conflict—until a final point of balance is reached: a resolution that seems less arbitrary and provisional than the invariably misleading moments of stasis within the body of the story. The construction of a plot consists of finding moments of stability, and then generating new narrative tensions that undo these moments—until the ending is reached.

What we call a "proper" ending of a novel is another equilibrium—one that, if it is properly designed, will have a recognizably different status. It will—this ending—persuade us that the tensions belonging to any difficult story have been sufficiently answered for. They have lost their power to effect further meaningful changes. They are held in check by the ending's capacity to seal everything in.

Endings in a novel confer a kind of liberty that life stubbornly denies us: to come to a full stop that is not death and discover exactly where we are in relation to the events leading to a conclusion. Here, the ending tells us, is the last segment of a hypothetical total experience—whose strength and authority we judge by the kind of clarity it brings, without undue coercion, to the events of the plot.

If an ending seems to be straining to align the conflicting forces of the narrative, we are likely to conclude that there are defects in the narrative structure, arising perhaps from the storyteller's lack of control or a confusion about what the story is capable of suggesting.

The pleasure of fiction is precisely that it moves to an ending. And an ending that satisfies is one that excludes. Whatever fails to connect with the story's closing pattern of illumination the writer assumes can be safely left out of the account.

A novel is a world with borders. For there to be completeness, unity, coherence, there must be borders. Everything is relevant in the journey we take within those borders. One could describe the story's end as a point of magical convergence for the shifting preparatory views: a fixed position from which the reader sees how initially disparate things finally belong together.

Further, the novel, by being an act of achieved form, is a process of understanding—whereas broken or insufficient form, in effect, does not know, wishes *not* to know, what belongs to it.

·

It is these two models that are now competing for our loyalty and attention.

There is an essential—as I see it—distinction between *stories*, on the one hand, which have, as their goal, an end, completeness, closure, and, on the other hand, *information*, which is always, by definition, partial, incomplete, fragmentary.

This parallels the contrasting narrative models proposed by *literature* and by *television*.

Literature tells stories. Television gives information.

Literature involves. It is the re-creation of human solidarity. Television (with its illusion of immediacy) distances—immures us in our own indifference.

The so-called stories that we are told on television satisfy our appetite for anecdote and offer us mutually canceling models of understanding. (This is reinforced by the practice of punctuating television narratives with advertising.) They implicitly affirm the idea that all information is potentially relevant (or "interesting"), that all stories are endless—or if they do stop, it is not because they have come to an end but, rather, because they have been upstaged by a fresher or more lurid or eccentric story.

By presenting us with a limitless number of nonstopped stories, the narratives that the media relate—the consumption of which has so dramatically cut into the time the educated public once devoted to reading—offer a lesson in amorality and detachment that is antithetical to the one embodied by the enterprise of the novel.

In storytelling as practiced by the novelist, there is always—as I have argued—an ethical component. This ethical component is not the truth, as opposed to the falsity of the chronicle. It is the model of completeness, of felt intensity, of enlightenment supplied by the story, and its resolution— which is the opposite of the model of obtuseness, of non- understanding, of passive dismay, and the consequent numb- ing of feeling, offered by our media-disseminated glut of unending stories.

•

Television gives us, in an extremely debased and *un-* truthful form, a truth that the novelist is obliged to suppress in the interest of the ethical model of understanding peculiar to the enterprise of fiction: namely, that the characteristic feature of our universe is that many things are happening at the same time. ("Time exists in order that it doesn't happen all at once . . . space exists so that it doesn't all happen to you.")

To tell a story is to say: *this* is the important story. It is to reduce the spread and simultaneity of everything to something linear, a path.

To be a moral human being is to pay, be obliged to pay, certain kinds of attention.

When we make moral judgments, we are not just saying that this is better than that. Even more fundamentally, we are saying that *this* is more *important* than *that*. It is to order the overwhelming spread and simultaneity of everything, at the price of ignoring or turning our backs on most of what is happening in the world.

The nature of moral judgments depends on our capacity for paying attention—a capacity that, inevitably, has its limits but whose limits can be stretched.

But perhaps the beginning of wisdom, and humility, is to acknowledge, and bow one's head, before the thought, the devastating thought, of the simultaneity of everything, and the incapacity of our moral understanding—which is also the understanding of the novelist—to take this in.

Perhaps this is an awareness that comes more easily to poets, who don't fully believe in storytelling. The supremely great early-twentieth-century Portuguese poet and prose writer, Fernando Pessoa, wrote in his prose summum, *The Book of Disquiet*:

> I've discovered that I'm always attentive to, and always thinking about two things at the same time. I suppose everyone is a bit like that . . . In my case the two realities that hold my attention are equally vivid. This is

what constitutes my originality. This, perhaps, is what
constitutes my tragedy, and what makes it comic.

Yes, everyone *is* a bit like that . . . but the awareness of the
doubleness of thinking is an uncomfortable position, very uncomfortable if held for long. It seems normal for people to reduce the complexity of what they are feeling and thinking,
and to close down the awareness of what lies outside their
immediate experience.

Is this refusal of an extended awareness, which takes in
more than is happening *right now, right here,* not at the heart
of our ever-confused awareness of human evil, and of the immense capacity of human beings to commit evil? Because there
are, incontestably, zones of experience that are not distressing,
that give joy, it becomes, perennially, a *puzzle* that there is so
much misery and wickedness. A great deal of narrative, and the
speculation that tries to free itself from narrative and become
purely abstract, inquires: Why does evil exist? Why do people
betray and kill each other? Why do the innocent suffer?

But perhaps the problem ought to be rephrased: Why is
evil not *everywhere?* More precisely, why is it somewhere—
but *not* everywhere? And what are we to do when it doesn't
befall us? When the pain that is endured is the pain of *others?*

Hearing the shattering news of the great earthquake
that leveled Lisbon on November 1, 1755, and (if historians
are to be believed) took with it a whole society's optimism
(but obviously, I *don't* believe that any society has only one
basic attitude), the great Voltaire was struck by the inability
to take in what happened elsewhere. "Lisbon lies in ruins,"
Voltaire wrote, "and here in Paris we dance."

One might suppose that in the twentieth century, in the

age of genocide, people would not find it either paradoxical or surprising that one can be so indifferent to what is happening simultaneously, elsewhere. Is it not part of the fundamental structure of experience that "now" refers to both "here" and "there"? And yet, I venture to assert, we are just as capable of being surprised—and frustrated by the inadequacy of our response—by the simultaneity of wildly contrasting human fates as was Voltaire two and a half centuries ago. Perhaps it is our perennial fate to be surprised by the simultaneity of events—by the sheer extension of the world in time and space. That here we are *here,* now prosperous, safe, unlikely to go to bed hungry or be blown to pieces this evening . . . while elsewhere in the world, right now . . . in Grozny, in Najaf, in the Sudan, in the Congo, in Gaza, in the favelas of Rio . . .

To be a traveler—and novelists are often travelers—is to be constantly reminded of the simultaneity of what is going on in the world, your world and the very different world you have visited and from which you have returned "home."

It is a beginning of a response to this painful awareness to say: it's a question of sympathy . . . of the limits of the imagination. You can also say that it's not "natural" to keep remembering that the world is so . . . extended. That while this is happening, that is also happening.

True.

But that, I would respond, is why we need fiction: to stretch our world.

.

Novelists, then, perform their necessary ethical task based on their right to a stipulated shrinking of the world as it really is—both in space and in time.

Characters in a novel act within a time that is already complete, where everything worth saving has been preserved—"washed free," as Henry James puts it in his preface to *The Spoils of Poynton*, "of awkward accretion" and aimless succession. All real stories are stories of someone's fate. Characters in a novel have intensely legible fates.

The fate of literature itself is something else. Literature as a story is full of awkward accretions, irrelevant demands, unpurposeful activities, uneconomical attention.

Habent sua fata fabulae, as the Latin phrase goes. Tales, stories, have their own fate. Because they are disseminated, transcribed, misremembered, translated.

Of course, one would not wish it otherwise. The writing of fiction, an activity that is necessarily solitary, has a destination that is necessarily public, communal.

Traditionally, all cultures are local. Culture implies barriers (for example, linguistic), distance, nontranslatability. Whereas what "the modern" means is, above all, the abolition of barriers, of distance; instant access; the leveling of culture— and, by its own inexorable logic the abolition, or revocation, of culture.

What serves "the modern" is standardization, homogenization. (Indeed, "the modern" is homogenization, standardization. The quintessential site of the modern is an airport; and all airports are alike, as all new modern cities, from Seoul to São Paulo, tend to look alike.) This pull toward homogenization cannot fail to affect the project of literature. The novel, which is marked by singularity, can only enter this system of maximum diffusion through the agency of translation, which, however necessary, entails a built-in distortion of what the novel is at the deepest level—which is not the communication of information, or even the telling of engaging stories, but the perpetuation of the project of literature itself, with its invitation to develop the kind of inwardness that resists the modern satieties.

To translate is to pass something across borders. But more and more the lesson of this society, a society that is "modern," is that there are no borders—which means, of course, no more or less than: no borders for the *privileged* sectors of society, which are more mobile geographically than ever before in human history. And the lesson of the hegemony of the mass media—television, MTV, the internet—is that there is only one culture, that what lies beyond borders everywhere is—or one day will be—just more of the same, with everyone on the planet feeding at the same trough of standardized entertainments and fantasies of eros and violence manufactured in the United States, Japan, wherever; with everyone enlightened by the same open-ended flow of bits of unfiltered (if, in fact, often censored) information and opinion.

That some pleasure, and some enlightenment, may be derived from these media is not to be denied. But I would argue that the mindset they foster and the appetites they feed are entirely inimical to the writing (production) and reading (consumption) of serious literature.

The transnational culture into which everyone who belongs to the capitalist consumer society—also known as the global economy—is being inducted is one that, in effect, makes literature irrelevant—a mere utility for bringing us what we already know—and can slot into the open-ended frameworks for the acquisition of information, and voyeuristic viewing at a distance.

At the Same Time: The Novelist and Moral Reasoning

Every novelist hopes to reach the widest possible audience, to pass as many borders as possible. But it is the novelist's job, I think, and I believe Nadine Gordimer agrees with me—it is the novelist's job to keep in mind the spurious cultural geography that is being installed at the beginning of the twenty-first century.

On the one hand, we have, through translation and through recycling in the media, the possibility of a greater and greater diffusion of our work. Space, as it were, is being vanquished. Here and there, we are told, are in constant contact with each other and are converging, mightily. On the other hand, the ideology behind these unprecedented opportunities for diffusion, for translation—the ideology now dominant in what passes for culture in modern societies—is designed to render obsolete the novelist's prophetic and critical, even subversive, task, and that is to deepen and sometimes, as needed, to *oppose* the common understandings of our fate.

Long live the novelist's task.

Acknowledgments

"An Argument About Beauty" appeared in *Daedalus* 131, no. 4 (Fall 2002).

"1926 ... Pasternak, Tsvetayeva, Rilke" was written as a preface to *Letters, Summer 1926: Boris Pasternak, Marina Tsvetayeva, Rainer Maria Rilke* (New York Review Books Classics, 2001). Prior to the book's publication, the essay appeared in the *Los Angeles Times Book Review*, August 12, 2001, with the title "The Sacred Delirium of Art."

"Loving Dostoyevsky" is the introduction to Leonid Tsypkin's *Summer in Baden-Baden* (New Directions, 2001). An earlier version appeared in *The New Yorker*, October 1, 2001.

"A Double Destiny: On Anna Banti's *Artemesia*" is the introduction to Anna Banti's *Artemisia* (Serpent's Tail, 2004). Prior to the book's publication, the essay appeared in *The London Review of Books*, October 9, 2003.

Acknowledgments

"Unextinguished: The Case for Victor Serge" is the introduction to Victor Serge's *The Case of Comrade Tulayev* (New York Review Books Classics, 2004). An abridged version appeared in *The Times Literary Supplement* on April 10, 2004.

"Outlandish: On Halldór Laxness's *Under the Glacier*" is the introduction to Halldór Laxness's *Under the Glacier* (Vintage, 2004). It also appeared in *The New York Times Book Review*, February 20, 2005.

"9.11.01" was written for *The New Yorker*. An edited version appeared in the "Talk of the Town" section on September 24, 2001. The original version has never before appeared in English.

"A Few Weeks After" was written in response to questions sent from Rome by Francesca Borrelli, a journalist on the staff of the Italian newspaper *il manifesto*, and was published in that paper on October 6, 2001. It has never before appeared in English.

"One Year After" was originally published as "War? Real Battles and Empty Metaphors" in *The New York Times*, Op-Ed page, September 10, 2002.

"Photography: A Little Summa" was written originally for *El Cultural* (July 10–16, 2003) and also appeared in *The Los Angeles Times Book Review* as "On Photography (The Short Course)" on July 27, 2003.

"Regarding the Torture of Others" was originally published in a slightly different form as "The Photographs *Are* Us" in *The New York Times Magazine*, May 23, 2004.

"The Conscience of Words," a speech given in Jerusalem on May 9, 2000,

Acknowledgments

on the occasion of the acceptance of the Jerusalem Prize, was published in *The Los Angeles Times Book Review* on June 10, 2001.

"The World as India," the 2002 St. Jerome Lecture on Literary Translation, appeared in *The Times Literary Supplement* on June 13, 2003.

"On Courage and Resistance," the keynote speech on the occasion of the presentation of the Rothko Chapel Oscar Romero Award to Ishai Menuchin, chairman of Yesh Gvul (There Is a Limit), the Israeli soldiers' movement for selective refusal, in 2003, appeared in *The Nation* on May 5, 2003.

"Literature Is Freedom" is a speech delivered at the Paulskirche, Frankfurt, on October 12, 2003, on the occasion of the acceptance of the Friedenspreis (Peace Prize) of the German Book Trade. Excerpts ran in *The Los Angeles Times Book Review* on October 26, 2003, and it was published in full by Winterhouse Editions in 2004.

"At the Same Time: The Novelist and Moral Reasoning," the first Nadine Gordimer Lecture, delivered in Cape Town and Johannesburg in March 2004, has never before appeared in print.